MERIDIAN

Crossing Aesthetics

Werner Hamacher

& David E. Wellbery

Editors

D1478335

Translated by
Peggy Kamuf

Stanford
University
Press

―――――

Stanford
California
1998

PSYCHOANALYZING

PSYCHOANALYZING

*On the Order of the Unconscious
and the Practice of the Letter*

Serge Leclaire

Psychoanalyzing
was originally published in French in 1968 as
*Psychanalyser: Un essai sur l'ordre de l'inconscient
et la pratique de la lettre*
© 1968 Editions du Seuil

Assistance for this translation was provided by
the French Ministry of Culture

Stanford University Press
Stanford, California

Printed in the United States of America

CIP data appear at the end of the book

Contents

PSYCHOANALYZING

§ 1 On the Ear with Which One Ought to Listen

One day the patient, stretched out on the couch, relates the following fantasy: a thief right out of melodrama, outrageously dressed up in mask, white gloves, and wide-brimmed hat pulled down over his eyes, breaks the display window of an art gallery and steals a painting that represents the very scene being enacted—in which a thief dressed in black breaks the display window of an art gallery—before being pulled into the downward spiral of the "black-wheel drive" with which this genre of film traditionally begins. The storyteller, who places himself in a corner of the scene, makes a show of indifference to it and slowly draws a cigarette from a red-and-white pack, a brand called Craven "A."

Taking advantage of the silence that sets in for a moment, and before the patient begins to comment on his fantasy, let us take up a position in the armchair, in the hidden retreat of the psychoanalyst's reflection. Right away he recognizes, but not without a faint uneasiness that stems from the feeling of familiarity, a typically obsessional phantasm. This only confirms, once more, his diagnostic point of view concerning this patient, and our psychoanalyst begins to muse about the variants on this phantasm he has already heard: the interrogation—puzzled, amused, fascinating, or even anxious—concerning the label on packages of cheese with the brand name "Laughing Cow," in which is represented a cow with long, dangling earrings made of two packages that naturally carry the same label, in which the same representation figures once again, and so on ad infinitum. There is also, muses our analyst, who at this hour is feeling hunger pangs, the many-faceted repetition of the label on Nicolas wines, where the delivery man, "Nectar," carries in each hand an array of bottles, all stamped with the same representation. In its purest form, our analyst also thinks, the phantasm is grounded in a real arrangement that produces this structure, when a subject is placed between two almost parallel mirrors: on each side the image is reproduced, back and front, in an indefinite series. But the analyst must not let himself get caught in these obsessional traps: he must hear instead what tends to get spoken in this fashion. The representation of the play with mirrors evokes for him the problem of identification and refers him back to the initial work of Jacques Lacan on "The Mirror Stage as Formative of the Function of the I."[1]

But what is he to do now with whatever he can still recall of this remarkable text? In the next moment, he wonders why he should let himself be fascinated in his turn by this evocation of the possible mirror plays. In this brief interval, the psychoanalyst feels himself slip along the floating thread of his attention; he reacts. Listening to the discourse of his patient, he must be attentive to the—unconscious—desire that is being spoken. That is the position he opted for by becoming a psychoanalyst: to listen to something other than the mere meaning of the words pronounced and to bring into the open the libidinal order they manifest. Besides, the very form of the discourse his patient has just addressed to him, that is, a fantasy, ought to lead him naturally in that direction—ought at least to be a sign that his interlocutor is following the rules of the analytic game by saying, without voluntary restraint, everything that comes to mind. Thus, the very fact that this patient, on this day, relates an oneiric fantasy, instead of enumerating one more time the inexorably logical series of his problems, shows a certain acquiescence to the terms chosen by his interlocutor. The psychoanalyst ought to be delighted about that, but he is not, for he senses that this fantasy hides intentions to seduce him, almost as if the patient had said, "Hey, here's a story you'll like! It's right up your alley." And, faced with this kind of connivance, the psychoanalyst begins to yearn for less devious or less informed patients, those who say right out, even before their interlocutor has opened his mouth, "Well, doctor, as for me, I don't believe a word of your stories."

So our psychoanalyst, in this brief interval of silence, barely the time of a dream, has let himself go on once more about his problems as a practitioner. But he gets hold of himself again and, with more sobriety and more precision, says to himself: "Okay, got it, I'm listening to his desire, and my hearing is not so bad because I've just perceived a seductive intention: if he's trying to seduce me, then no doubt it's in order to 'possess' me, take advantage of me, or, more surely still, neutralize me, because he's afraid of what I might do or say. I am back on solid and familiar ground. The fear is certainly the fear of castration, which arises there as a consequence of certain oedipal desires; that's natural since my patient knows in a more or less confused fashion that, precisely, I'm listening to his desires, and thus he's only a step away from imagining that I'm the one who arouses his desires, that I am in turn the seducer."

At this point, peace settles over the armchair. Our psychoanalyst has found once again the two major points of reference that help him to sustain his chosen position under all circumstances: Oedipus and castration.

But the euphoria is short lived. This time the silence is prolonged and stretches almost into the interval of a second dream. The analyst marks the interval, finally opening his mouth in turn, with an evasive "yes" that is more questioning than approving. There is no immediate response from the patient, which leaves his close-mouthed interlocutor free to pursue his own musings on his present, very present, practice. What else can one say for the moment other than this yes-in-waiting? No doubt it would be premature, and even risky, to expose the patient's seductive intention (even though our analyst plays with the idea), given that the recommended and preferred practice is to intervene "at the level of the transference," that is, at the level of the desire that actually pre-

sents itself in the context of the session. At this point, as if the psychoanalyst had been thinking aloud, the patient answers him as
someone who is aware of the rudiments of analytic theory and
practice, as are most people today who undergo an analysis.

So the analysand begins to speak once again, putting an end to a
silence that lasted no more than two minutes. Not without some
bitterness he recounts how this daydream is no doubt related to
the lengthy visit he recently paid to Iolas, an art gallery, where he
had particularly admired and dreamed of acquiring a painting by
Magritte. Unfortunately, the cost of his treatment excludes, for the
moment, any purchase of this sort, a constraint that might very
well make him quite violently angry, especially if he started thinking that the analyst, by contrast, could acquire a painting of this
sort, using, precisely, the fees he receives. Right away he adds,
moreover, that, while in the waiting room he had the opportunity
to think about how he could easily walk off with one of the art re-
views or steal one of the small statues exhibited in a case, or even,
more exquisitely, break a vase displayed there. Then he continues
these violent evocations in silence.

So now, here is our analyst, completely gratified. Not only does
the patient spontaneously offer, with his associations, the effective
presence of this transferential dimension by bringing forth the agitated emotions he feels in the context of the treatment and with
regard to the analyst,[2] but also what he has just said illustrates or
confirms the sequence well known to practitioners, namely, frustration, aggression, and regression.[3] In sum, the analyst recognizes
here what he has been taught in the most academic fashion: the
analytic situation, which should in no way respond to the patient's
demands, is necessarily felt by him to be "frustrating,"[4] and as such
it is bound to arouse his aggressive reactions when, prevented by
the treatment's protocol from satisfying his impulses,[5] he has no
choice but to "regress" to more archaic modes of reaction.

Although the analyst cannot explain this academic sequence to
his patient, he also cannot avoid recognizing in it a familiar concatenation. If he is still a novice, or somewhat naive, he will feel a
certain satisfaction, inasmuch as this reference to a set of events de-

scribed by the classical authors gives him the sense that, in this case, he has done what had to be done. But concerned, as he was just a moment before, "to interpret in the transference," he will not miss the opportunity to do so here, and indeed everything compels him to go in that direction. He has not forgotten the patient's stories about himself as a child, all in a rage because he could not find among his father's things the key to a desk drawer where he knew a revolver was hidden or, in the same series of memories, reveling in the manipulation of a lighter that he took from a more easily accessible bureau. Furthermore, our analyst was attentive to the mention of the name of the gallery, Iolas, and heard its oddity, the way in which it is the anagram of Laïos [Laius]. There is thus no more doubt about the murderous intentions of the potential (or shelved) Oedipus harbored by this patient (like every patient); this Oedipus poses merely the additional enigma of the inversion of *Io* and *la*, in this context.

Thus, the opportunity presents itself here, "in the transference," to bring out the still-current character of the patient's feelings of violent rivalry with his father regarding the possession of a symbolic object, which is as real and tangible as it is imaginary and infinitely mysterious. Our analyst, however—who wants to be careful about planting suggestions in his interlocutor and, therefore, saying too much (all the more so because he thinks there is a lot to say)—limits himself to an altogether classical remark, the barest minimum of what might be strictly called an interpretation: "One must note that you have on occasion expressed—and silenced—violent feelings toward me, concerning objects you covet, and that these feelings recall the powerless rage you used to display when your father, or on one occasion his desk, resisted your desires"—whereupon he adds, by way of insinuation, "What is it, then, you wanted to take?"

This remark is correct and in keeping with the most academic rules, but it is just barely interpretive if one leaves aside its insinuations. The analyst has in fact been overly timid, and he will quickly see the effects of his discourse. To be sure, the "aggressive" feelings of his patient are encouraged by this discourse to manifest themselves but perhaps not exactly in the manner one might wish. They now have a good opportunity to leave their true object in the shadows, even as they pour forth in irony, amply nourished by the substance of the remark.

"So then," he in effect says to his interlocutor, all the while feigning surprise, "apparently I really felt hostility toward my father, who prevented me from stealing his precious goods. Let me guess: it must be a matter not only of his revolver—why not just say his penis—but also and above all his wife, my mother, whence one must infer that I wanted to possess my mother. What a discovery! . . . and what a mockery!" It is quite obvious that even before beginning analysis the patient knew, as everyone today knows, that he had experienced an oedipal situation. Thus, what the analyst tells him is as true as it is derisive and finds its only support in the notion of the privilege awarded to the present, which should be underscored by the emphasis the remark placed on the current, transferential character of the aggressive feelings. But it is no less obvious that the patient, in this instance, is justified in feeling that his speech has been overlaid with a kind of pre-comprehensive grid in which everything that might occur to him will be made to fit necessarily and in an organized fashion around the model of Oedipus and castration, according to a few—in fact very few—stereotypes. Moreover, with the momentum of his aggressive irony, he is led to drive the point home so as to confound his interlocutor. He underscores the "painting" component in his oneiric fantasy, inasmuch as it is a second-degree representation of the scene of the daydream in which it is the focal point, and he gets some pleasure out of imagining what Michel Foucault in the analyst's place would have done with this "representation of representation" at the time he was writing "Las Meninas."[6]

Letting himself worship briefly at the altar of the well-known principle according to which the patient is always wrong, our analyst wants to hear in these last words only a manifestation of the patient's resistance to the impact of some truth that has gotten too close to his unconscious. And yet, whatever the case, whether the analyst persists in thinking that he has put his finger on it, or whether he acknowledges that he missed the sore point in question, he still has to specify the nature of this sensitive point, for it cannot be "aggressivity," "rivalry," or the "fear of castration" in the general sense of the truth of those concepts. The best thing for the psychoanalyst to do in this circumstance, once he has gotten over the irritation he is not supposed to feel, is to return to the patient's speech. And it happens that, even in his eloquent, ironic outburst, which elicited Foucault as analyst, the analysand put emphasis on one element of the daydream—the painting. Everything, therefore, invites one to question this focal point; up to now, the patient has only referred to it by its author, Magritte, and alluded vaguely to its subject, a woman's body. "Well then, exactly," the analyst inserts in an interrogative tone, "what about this painting?"

It is a woman made up of assembled stones, like a monument; in her body there is the cut out form of a soaring, immobile bird, a frame through which one can see the sea. It is an amazing composition that invites an outpouring of possible interpretations, which all converge in fascination on this vanishing point of flight over the sea. But this composition turns out to be even more surprising when one realizes that it is not the work of Magritte but in fact of the patient, who has reworked in his own way some of the painter's familiar themes: he could have borrowed the woman from the statue of the *Flowers of Evil*, or perhaps from the trunk of Venusian stone on the beach, titled *When the Hour Chimes*; the assembled stones can be found massive in the prison wall (on which is inscribed a table covered with a white cloth) of *The Amiable Truth*; as for the bird, it is an exact, inverted figuration of *The Idol*, a petrified bird soaring at the edge of water and a rocky shore.[7]

With this window that overlooks the sea [*mer*, homonym of *mère*, mother], cut out in a monument-woman or prison, the analysis opens onto the dimension of its singular truth. Now one must follow it through the unexpected meanderings of its detours. The broken glass of the daydream leads the patient to recall a fall through the frame of a greenhouse and the deep cut that scarred him. But our analyst is not in a hurry, this time, to conclude his understanding, or to close down his hearing, by resorting to the term of castration, and he wisely allows speech to continue. This reciprocal effraction of the glass surface and at the same time the body is an active commentary on the cutout opened in the stone wall of the prison-woman's body. And then there follows an evocation of architectural compositions; their masses, volumes, and openings: these windows of Magritte's paintings revive the memory of a travel photo in which one can see, very clearly drawn, the regular openings in the peaceful square mass of the bell tower of the church at Cravant.[8]

Listening now with a less prejudiced ear, the analyst is not taken in by the fascination with the play of openings and can hear the name of Cravant literally as a gallicized reprise—or one that obeys the "A"[9]—of the Craven "A" cigarettes from the dream. Not without "reason," moreover, for the patient, in order to convey the comic effect produced by the doubled scene of the painting in the daydream, had repeated several times that it was "crevant,"[10] which right away leads to other "crevantes" situations with an analogous structure wherein the unconscious term is unveiled unexpectedly and provokes laughter, at the limit of anxiety.[11] For the interpretation here, whose time should not be missed, two words are enough: "à crever," launched like an echo, are words that are going to touch on the patient's most sensitive spot, unveiling for an instant his most secret, unconscious intention to crush or puncture, that is, "crever," the maternal body. In this form, the generality of the aggressive movement already identified in its relative nonspecificity is suddenly specified, in the most singular fashion, as an intention to break into violently, even to destroy, the space that is set out around the inaccessible treasure supposedly hidden there.[12]

Today, we are no longer surprised by the extraordinary situation in which seemingly the sole concern of the appointed interlocutor is never to show himself at every point where he is expected. From the first, the psychoanalyst hides from his patient's view and, if the latter assumes him to be interested in the subtle, oedipal story being recounted, he will retain only the stumblings of language. In the reverse pattern, if the psychoanalyzed "offers" his listener a "nice" *lapsus*, the psychoanalyst will have an ear only for the sequence scanned by the slip. Things have gotten to the point that, at its most extreme, the analyst's art seems to be that of expecting nothing, and consequently in today's world he does not lack for well-informed patients who reply from the first that they too expect nothing! One may imagine the particular difficulty involved in the subtle complicity of this hiding game.

What is the point, however, of this systematic flight from all the discursive traps set out by the patient?

That is a question we cannot avoid, and our whole undertaking here will be devoted to conveying the order of truth that is called upon to manifest itself in the psychoanalytic situation.

Psychoanalyzing, as we have just seen, is a rather discomforting practice. If one relies on what one thinks one knows about psychic structure or treatment technique, then these landmarks soon turn out to be inoperative when invoked, for the simple reason, for example, that the patient shares, more or less, this supposed knowledge. If one takes no account of the importance of this common implicit reference to knowledge, then psychoanalysis very quickly becomes installed in a misrecognition of the fact of this theoretical complicity and ends up producing effects of almost total enclosure, not to say alienation. One need only imagine the kind of laughable exchange of misunderstandings that could take place between patient and analyst, each of them referring to the image he has of the notion of resistance. One of them does so in order to infer that his speech is constantly hampered by inevitable resistance; the other in order to pretend to discover that the speech (or the silence) of his interlocutor is merely resistance to other avowals, unless (if he is more subtle but no less stubborn) he exposes a resistance at work in the very avowal of a feeling of resistance. And yet, it is quite certain that one cannot, all the same, impugn the solidity of these technical references—resistance, transference—just as one cannot seriously contest the necessary recourse to the fundamental structures of Oedipus and castration.

Conversely, if one lets oneself be guided by the flash of intuition, one quickly realizes (provided one keeps a minimum of lucidity) that such supposed intuition is most often nothing but the projection of a privileged element of the analyst's knowledge or his unconscious phantasm. Thus, when our analyst begins to underscore that the cutout in the painting figures the opening or the frame of the phantasm, he pretends to forget, at that moment, how it is precisely with the example of paintings by Magritte that Lacan had, at one time, illustrated the structure of phantasm. At that point, he is using this scholarly reminiscence under the cover of an intuition.[13] At a still more radical level of critique, one must indeed admit that there seems to be no absolute guarantee that the privilege granted to the patient's "crevant" (just to stay with the text of our example) does not arise from a particularly invested term in the unconscious phantasms of the analyst. Nothing guarantees this other than, up to a certain point, the psychoanalysis that the practitioner is supposed to have undergone before gaining access to the armchair.

In the accounts of analyses left to us by Freud we find signs of these profound difficulties inherent in psychoanalytic practice. Thus, in the analysis of Dora, Freud acknowledges in a note added in 1923, more than twenty years after the treatment, that he had not heard what his patient had been saying about the homosexual love she felt for Frau K.: "The longer the interval of time that separates me from the end of this analysis, the more probable it seems to me that the fault in my technique lay in this omission: I failed to discover in time and to inform the patient that her homosexual (gynaecophilic) love for Frau K. was the strongest unconscious current in her mental life. . . . Before I had learnt the importance of the homosexual current of feeling in psychoneurotics, I was often brought to a standstill in the treatment of my cases or found myself in complete perplexity" (*SE* 7: 120; *GW* 5: 284). No doubt these difficulties of treatment are due to the fact that, as Freud writes, he had not yet "learnt the importance of the homosexual current of feeling in psychoneurotics," but one may add, by way of complement, that because he was more concerned at the time with testing, through the transference, the truth and universality of the girl's incestuous love for her father,[14] Freud did not recognize the homosexual tendencies, or rather he did not pay them all the attention one might have wished.

The influence of a theoretical concern on the course of the treatment is likewise noticeable in the history of the "Wolf Man." Already in the introduction to this case study there is a recognition of this influence in the form of a disavowal: "Readers may at all events rest assured that I myself am only reporting what I came upon as an independent experience, uninfluenced by my expectation."[15] But the aware reader realizes quickly that all the material relating to the primal scene,[16] which forms the essential part of the observation, was obtained "under the inexorable pressure" (*SE* 17: 11; *GW* 12: 34) of a date set by Freud, which already manifests the analyst's hopeful expectation that he be given something. In the context of this treatment, it turns out that Freud's expectation can be located very precisely: he hopes to obtain from his patient supplementary proof, which would finally preclude any challenge, of the existence of a kernel of reality around which neurosis is formed.[17] And it seems quite certain that the patient's narration, or reconstruction, of the primal scene meets Freud's expectation very precisely.

Finally, one finds in this same analysis of the Wolf Man an example that clearly demonstrates the way in which decisive representations of the analyst's unconscious can interfere with the conduct of the analysis. Not long before the date set for the end of the treatment, the patient takes up again with Freud the still-enigmatic childhood memory of the great fear he felt on the day a beautiful butterfly with yellow stripes, which he had been chasing, landed gently on a flower. For the moment, we will not relate the analysis of this memory but only one of the ideas that occurred to Freud in order to attempt the beginning of an interpretation: "I will not conceal the fact that at the time I put forward the possibility that the yellow stripes on the butterfly had reminded him of similar stripes upon a piece of clothing worn by some women" (*SE* 17: 89; *GW* 12: 123). Although one must note that this suggestion encoun-

tered no echo coming from the patient, it is interesting to point
out what a yellow (-striped) dress represents for Freud. We find it
in the article "Screen Memories," in which the central argument is
constituted by an autobiographical fragment.[18] The yellow dress,
which was, he specifies, a somewhat brownish yellow, is the one
worn by a childhood friend, Gisela Fluss, when he saw her again
at the age of seventeen and fell passionately, though secretly, in love
with her: "I can remember quite well that for a long time after-
wards I was affected by the yellow colour of the dress she was wearing when we first met, whenever I saw the same colour anywhere
else" (*SE* 3: 313; *GW* 1: 540).

These few faithful fragments of that practice we call analysis
show that, in fact, the rules of analytic attention are impossible to
uphold. In his "Recommendations to Physicians Practising Psycho-
Analysis," Freud writes:

> The technique . . . consists simply in not directing one's notice to any-
> thing in particular and in maintaining the same "evenly-suspended at-
> tention" (as I have called it) in the face of all that one hears. In this
> way we spare ourselves a strain on our attention . . . and we avoid a
> danger which is inseparable from the exercise of deliberate attention.
> For as soon as anyone deliberately concentrates his attention to a cer-
> tain degree, he begins to select from the material before him; one
> point will be fixed in his mind with particular clearness and some
> other will be correspondingly disregarded, and in making this selec-
> tion he will be following his expectations or inclinations. This, how-
> ever, is precisely what must not be done. In making the selection, if
> he follows his expectations he is in danger of never finding anything
> but what he already knows; and if he follows his inclinations he will
> certainly falsify what he may perceive. It must not be forgotten that
> the things one hears are for the most part things whose meaning is
> only recognized later on.
>   It will be seen that the rule of giving equal notice to everything is
> the necessary counterpart to the demand made on the patient that he
> should communicate everything that occurs to him without criticism
> or selection. If the doctor behaves otherwise, he is throwing away
> most of the advantage which results from the patient's obeying the

"fundamental rule of psycho-analysis." The rule for the doctor may be expressed: "He should withhold all conscious influences from his capacity to attend and give himself over completely to his 'unconscious memory.'" Or, to put it purely in terms of technique: "He should simply listen, and not bother about whether he is keeping anything in mind." (*SE* 12: 112; *GW* 8: 377–78)

Thus, in this recommended state of floating attention, without relying on some established order of preference, the psychoanalyst must be able to receive what the patient says in the course of the session, after having been invited to let things come without discrimination. This is the situation in all its paradox, which may readily be compared to some mad undertaking in which a blind navigator without a compass invites his passenger to take the wind whichever way it blows. Quite obviously, this is an untenable position, and Freud was the first to say so. Indeed, who could ever seriously claim to succeed in erasing all his prejudices, giving up all the secret preferences that constitute the order of his world, his very way of seeing, feeling, loving, listening? With such a claim, the severe psychoanalyst evokes, in the worst case, the schizophrenic's world from which all possible order vanishes and, in the best case, of the obsessive endlessly employed in contesting the established order so as to give himself the illusion of overcoming his attachment to it. Doubtless it is not just the psychiatrist who would be ready to denounce as impossible and absurd what is commonly called the neutrality of the analyst; at the extreme, it would be easy to denounce the systematic as well as illusory character of a position that aims to be totally noncritical. One need not have practiced long to know that there are patients who need no invitation to apply very systematically the noncritical principle of the rule of free association with the sole purpose of never saying anything, just as one could imagine that there are psychoanalysts who, applying the letter of the law of floating attention, make it their duty never to hear anything.

In fact, this neutrality of the analyst aims only to describe a certain affective or libidinal position, since, as everyone knows who has ever been around a psychoanalyst, your average Freudian is anything but the totally unprejudiced scholar. One could even say that by becoming an analyst he agreed to take on new prejudices and that he very often presents himself as someone who has taken a position, who never wants to listen to the reasoning that supports his interlocutor's discourse, and who seems very adept at the side-stepping game, which he plays with a remarkable flair for the systematic. Thus, if you arrive for your appointment on time, early, or late, and if in trying to respond to his questioning insinuations you say that it was, respectively, "just" out of politeness, out of prudence, or by accident, he will nevertheless think silently or even out loud that you are obsessive if you are on time, anxious if you are early, and deceitfully aggressive if you were held up by a breakdown of the subway. In a word, the psychoanalyst can never be found where you expect him and, just as he sidesteps the traps of the face-to-face in the arrangement of the furniture, he seems bent on never answering there where he is questioned. Correlatively, everyone knows that there is nevertheless one place where one is more or less certain to run into the psychoanalyst: at the crossroads that is the place of the missing phallus,[19] there where any discourse whatsoever can be interpreted in terms of sexual value. Everyone will agree that we have here a prejudice of the first order.

It cannot be denied that sex is indeed the cornerstone of psychoanalysis. Whether it is denounced by detractors, extolled—as if that were necessary—by enthusiasts, recognized, or at least accepted, which is to say fundamentally misrecognized, sex remains, in its irreducible flash of light, the psychoanalyst's order of reference. Moreover, if there were no law, how could the analyst make the connection, either right away or after the fact as Freud recommends, between elements gathered in the course of the sessions?[20] It is obvious that the reconstruction called interpretation can only be done by following a certain logic. To announce or denounce this logic as libidinal and sexual neither suffices in the least to discredit it nor takes the place of a proof that accredits it.

One may thus see the double requirement imposed on the psychoanalyst: on the one hand, he must have at his disposal a system of reference, a theory that can permit him to order the mass of material he gathers without prior discrimination; on the other hand, he must set aside any system of reference precisely to the extent that adherence to a set of theories necessarily leads him, whether he likes it or not, to privilege certain elements. One may ask whether the reference to the fact of sex, which is central for psychoanalysis, is sufficient to guarantee respect for this double requirement and, if it is, one must be prepared to explain how.

Thus, a question is posed that cannot be avoided: *how can one conceive a theory of psychoanalysis that does not annul, in the very fact of its articulation, the fundamental possibility of its practice?* It is a matter, as we have just seen, on the one hand, of upholding firmly the urgent necessity for the analyst to give up all his prejudices, to "eliminat[e] his pre-existing convictions . . . thoroughly,"[21] so as to keep his ear absolutely open; on the other hand, it is a matter of holding on just as firmly, not to the privilege of some obscure origin, but to the very principle of an open logic that is, as we will see, a logic that takes account of the facts of sex and *jouissance.*[22]

Between the lines here one may glimpse what makes for both the necessity and the difficulty of a true theory of psychoanalysis. This theory is necessary if one is not to let psychoanalysis be practiced under the exclusive sign of intuition (or the "sixth sense" as clinicians say). Otherwise, there is the risk of seeing analysis go the way of a kind of phantasmatization-for-two that would place it, by this very fact, outside any possible order as well as any analysis in its formal implication. Just imagine what would have happened if Freud had been less objectively scientific and less clear-sighted as to the sources of his intuition (an intuition, moreover, that he said he distrusted)[23] and had insisted on the hypothesis of the yellow-striped dress: without a doubt, a patient as manifestly docile as the Wolf Man would have ended up retrieving a true, or false, memory that satisfied his interlocutor. In an ultimate paradox, this would have even probably been enough to allow some progress in the analysis all the same, through one of those detours around an impasse that it willingly follows.

Conversely, this theory is difficult to establish because adapting psychoanalysis to a complete formalization (which is what the common effort to theorize naturally aims to achieve) would have to exclude from its field, ipso facto, the very possibility of analysis in search of extreme singularity. Thus, clearly all it would have taken was a little insistence by the analyst on the theory of the castration complex, and he could have convinced the patient who visited the Iolas gallery of the universal pertinence of this dimension. Here again, no doubt, the treatment would have gained some momentum in this fashion, but it also would have lost, for a time, access to the singular and very sensitive insistence of a major element of his unconscious, the term "crever."

Only a true theory can advance a formalization that maintains, without reducing it, the domain of singularity; the always recurring difficulty of psychoanalysis, which no institution will ever be able to resolve, derives from the fact that it is vulnerable, on the one hand, to the degradation of a closed systematization and, on the other, to the anarchy of intuitive processes. The theory of psychoanalysis has to keep both of these pitfalls simultaneously in view, to avoid them but also to orient itself by them.

The rigorousness of unconscious desire, its logic, is revealed only to whoever respects simultaneously these two apparently contradictory requirements that are order and singularity. Let us now try to examine how Freud approached them.

§ 2 Unconscious Desire:
With Freud, Reading Freud

Freud taught that dreams ought to be deciphered like rebuses. He attempted thereby to illustrate the fundamental fact of a very clear distinction between the manifest content of the dream or the literal text of the rebus, on the one hand, and the latent content or the dream-thoughts, on the other: "the dream-content seems like a transcript of the dream-thoughts into another mode of expression."[1] He immediately adds, although without insisting on it, that this other mode of expression is not in any way sufficient in itself and has to be referred to (or is constituted by) the set of dream-thoughts: "another mode of expression whose characters and systematic laws it is our business to discover by comparing the original and the translation." "Suppose," Freud continues,

> I have a picture-puzzle, a rebus, in front of me. It depicts a house with a boat on its roof, a single letter of the alphabet, the figure of a running man whose head has been conjured away, and so on. Now I might be misled into raising objections and declaring that the picture as a whole and its component parts are nonsensical. A boat has no business to be on the roof of a house, and a headless man cannot run. Moreover, the man is bigger than the house; and if the whole picture is intended to represent a landscape, letters of the alphabet are out of place in it since such objects do not occur in nature. But obviously we can only form a proper judgment of the rebus if we put aside criticisms such as these of the whole composition and its parts and if, in-

stead, we try to replace each separate element by a syllable or word that can be represented by that element in some way or other. (*SE* 4: 277–78; *GW* 2: 284)

Freud nevertheless registers a kind of surprise, or admiration, when a patient, taking his theory at its word, proposes to him an immediate interpretation of a dream: this interlocutor takes the dream "my uncle kisses me in an automobile" to be a rebus and translates it as "auto-eroticism," which Freud admits he would not have thought of.

All the same, this seems to answer the question we were asking about the definition of a rule for listening: just as the dream demands that it be heard and understood as a rebus, in which the manifest content ought to lead us to the latent thoughts, likewise the patient's speech can be considered as an apparent and misleading text that masks true secret thoughts. This is, to be sure, a simple and convenient view whose minimal correctness explains the high favor in which it is commonly held. No one can actually say that he forgot his umbrella or lost his lighter, both of which habitually figure in sexual rebuses, without provoking right away the knowing smile of his interlocutor, who has become a hermeneut for the occasion. Obviously, this simplistic conception, which gives excessive weight to a correct but partial point of view, cannot suffice to direct in any real way the analyst's attention, a point that becomes clear as soon as one looks closely at the rebus analogy. In fact, it is quite clear that, in most cases, the text of the rebus, or the manifest content of the dream, is not translated by the mere formulation of the rebus's figures into words. Or, more exactly, this translation into words encounters a supplementary problem: one must have some clue as to the nature of the "latent thoughts" before an expression of the enigma can be organized into words.

Let us imagine, for example, a rebus that represents a stretch of ocean on which figure two glasses, literally "deux verres à la mer." This very simple composition, extrapolated in these terms, allows for a whole series of possible translations. According to the most obvious wordplay, it might be an evocation of a "painting by Vermeer," certainly a necessary interpretation if the context includes some "Delft blue." But, in fact, it is rare that the clue is as clear-cut as this, and more often one has to continue listening for one or more clues that will indicate how to choose among the variants of the elements presented: "le vert et l'amer," "le deux et la paire," "le père et la mère," "le pervers et l'âme errante," "le boire à la mère et la mer à boire," all of which terms figure virtually in the dream-rebus.[2] Among these several possibilities, it is not easy to choose the correct arrangement that will guide a true interpretation, unless at least one term of the latent thoughts can be identified. As one can imagine, such an identification will be arbitrary if the rules presiding over the organization of these latent thoughts are not clearly recognized. In other words, this choice is only possible through reference to the unconscious order in which it is produced.

Because of its simplicity and the immediate acceptance it incites, however, the easy-to-handle distinction between manifest and latent seems to conceal in itself the seeds of useless problems where the edges of the unconscious fact vanish. Thus, one can catch oneself hastily considering the manifest text as a simple screen meant to veil the truth of the latent text. This is the naive and very widespread way of distinguishing what is really supposed to be true from its misleading expression. In fact, the mode in which the two texts are related cannot become apparent until one has identified the alphabet that constitutes the writing of the latent thoughts because, as we have just seen, this alphabet differs from the more accessible and familiar one that constitutes the manifest text. The latent thoughts are inscribed as *unconscious desires* and, without any doubt, it is only through a rigorous interrogation of the Freudian notion of unconscious desire, in all its radical novelty, that one can hope to situate among other notions the didactic distinction between the latent and the manifest. Above all, however, the only way one can hope to enter into the heart of the psychoanalytic experience is by developing the extraordinary fertility of this aphorism: *a dream is the fulfillment of a wish.*

〜

To do this, there is no surer road than Freud's procedure in the analysis of his own dreams inasmuch as it also constitutes the very invention of psychoanalysis. Doubtless, this road is sure, but it is also arduous, long, and winding, as we are going to find out: such is, in Freud's own words, the *royal road* leading to the unconscious.

Two dreams, which became centerpieces of the *Traumdeutung*'s structure, will provide our point of departure in this quite exceptional reading, where the reality of desire is revealed at the same time in its singularity and its universality.[3] On first analysis, the dream of *Irma's injection* (July 1895) and that of the *botanical monograph* (March 1898) both manifest the dreamer's great ambition and bring out a basic intention to protest and exculpate. Covering a three-year interval, they point to the persistence or even, in Freud's own terms, the perennial nature of unconscious desire.

On the night of July 23–24, 1895, Freud dreams of the injection given to Irma, the first dream to be submitted to a detailed analysis (*SE* 4: 107; *GW* 2: 111). It is a plea for the defense in which he exculpates and justifies himself: he is not the one responsible for the incomplete recovery of his patient Irma, of which he has just been informed by his friend Otto with, it seemed to him, a hint of reproach. The dream is also a protest, which takes a vengeful turn when it insinuates that it is not he but also Otto who has perhaps acted negligently. The dreamer affirms finally the correctness of his opinion by reproaching Irma—and no doubt along with her many others—for not having yet "accepted his solution," that is, psychoanalysis.

This dream about Irma is also and above all a proof Freud gives himself of the truth of his hypothesis, which is why it will serve as the inaugural demonstration in his book. We know, in fact, that Freud was looking forward at this time to his vacation so he could advance his projects and verify his latest ideas about the theory of the neuroses. In particular, he wished to study normal psychic phenomena and submit to a decisive verification the hypothesis that dreams are, in their own way, the fulfillment of a wish. Perhaps, he hypothesizes, dreams are always like those of his friend Rudi who, in order not to have to wake up and get out of bed, dreams that he is already at the hospital where he must go for work?[4] These were, in very quick outline, Freud's scientific preoccupations in the month of July 1895.

The dream of Irma's injection, therefore, reveals to him, in more than one respect, that it is the fulfillment of a wish. Not only, as we've seen, does it accomplish the desire to exculpate him, but also and most of all the analysis reveals the dream to be the satisfaction of a fundamental desire to unveil that which is hidden, to violate unexplored regions, to steal secrets, to be the hero who steps over the frontiers of knowledge: to put it in a word, the desire to transgress.

It is indeed an exploit that Freud feels he has accomplished by dreaming and then by interpreting the scene of Irma's injection. He acknowledges this five years later, during the dark summer that followed the failure of the publication of *Interpretation of Dreams*, when he wrote in a letter to his friend Fliess:

"Do you suppose that some day a marble tablet will be placed on the house, inscribed with these words:

> In this house on July 24th, 1895
> the Secret of Dreams was revealed to
> Dr. Sigmund Freud

At this moment I see little prospect of it" (*OP* 137).

And yet we can say retrospectively, it was on this night of dreams that the sentence summing up his discovery got written: *"When the work of interpretation has been completed, we perceive that a dream is the fulfillment of a wish"* (*SE* 4: 121; *GW* 2: 126).

In *The Interpretation of Dreams*, before revealing this major stage along his way, Freud writes: "I must ask the reader to make my interests his for quite a while, and to plunge along with me, into the minutest details of my life" (*SE* 4: 106; *GW* 2: 110). We have alluded to the nature of "theoretical" preoccupations at the time of the dream, but it is more difficult and may seem more risky, even indiscreet, to interest oneself, as one does in analysis, in "the minutest details" of someone's life. As Didier Anzieu has already emphasized,[5] it does appear that Freud's principal preoccupation at this time was related to the problems of conception or fecundity, to be understood in the sense of procreation as well as creation. Martha, his wife, was expecting a sixth child, who seems not to have been particularly wanted, but who would nevertheless turn out to be Anna, the only psychoanalyst among his children. "If you have really solved the problem of conception," he writes to Fliess, "the only thing left for you to do is to make up your mind what kind of marble you prefer. For me your discovery is a few months too late, but it may come in useful next year. In any case, I am consumed with curiosity to hear more about it" (*OP* 24). One may note here incidentally the appearance of a first form of the marble tablet fantasy, meant for his friend, but already ambiguous because in this allusive form it evokes equally a sign of glory and a tombstone. Above all, however, there is a recognition in these lines of a consuming desire to know more about the problem of conception. Beneath the question of psychological theory, which preoccupies Freud to be sure, we see appear already his veritable passion as a solver of enigmas. Furthermore, after the publication of *The Interpretation of Dreams* he will find himself, like another Oedipus at Colonus, "blind and groping about."

The desire that haunts him, before the dream of Irma's injection comes along to fulfill it in a way, seems therefore to be *the desire to force open the secret of desire,* to unveil the reality of sexual life. With the Irma dream, the envelope of mystery, ignorance, and denial veiling the truth of desire is lifted before him. We can already glimpse the roots of a phantasm of Freud's if we stop to consider the terms he imagines chiseled on the marble tablet, in particular the verb *enthüllen,* to unveil, reveal. It is composed of *Hülle,* envelope, integument, mortal coil, and the prefix *ent-,* which indicates separation, origin, deliverance, evasion, "often with the additional idea of secrecy" (says our German dictionary). Freud fantasizes this marble tablet, glory and death, for himself, not without having first meant it for Fliess.

It is in the same context of the dialogue with Fliess that the dream of the botanical monograph will be elaborated.

Beginning in February 1898, Freud devotes himself to the writing of the *Traumdeutung*: "Self-analysis has been dropped in favour of the dream book" (*OP* 83). Toward March he arrives at the second chapter, precisely the one in which he relates the dream of Irma's injection. One day, at the beginning of this month, he receives a friendly and encouraging letter from Fliess, who writes: "I am very much occupied with your dream-book. I see it lying finished before me and I see myself turning over its pages" (*SE* 4: 172; *GW* 2: 175). The next night Freud has the dream of the botanical monograph: "I had written a monograph on a certain plant. The book lay before me and I was at the moment turning over a folded coloured plate. Bound up in each copy there was a dried specimen of the plant, as though it had been taken from a herbarium" (*SE* 4: 169; *GW* 2: 175). This dream, to which Freud will refer repeatedly (*SE* 4: 191, 281, 305; 5: 467; *GW* 2: 197, 286, 310; 3: 470), has once again, he writes, like the dream of Irma's injection, the character of a justification, a plea for the defense: to all those who, like his friend Königstein on the evening before the dream, reproach him for giving too much free rein to his hobbies, he replies with the dream that his research is bearing fruit.

As we know and as the analysis of the dream recalls, Freud had come very close to earning recognition for the discovery of the analgesic properties of cocaine. He had written a monograph "on the coca-plant," which appeared in July 1884 and which, he writes, had drawn the attention of other researchers to the anesthetic properties of cocaine. "I had myself indicated this application of the alkaloid in my published paper, but I had not been thorough enough to pursue the matter further" (*SE* 4: 170; *GW* 2: 176). A little later, at the end of July, impatient to rejoin his fiancée, Martha, he had left it to his friend Königstein to pursue the experiment. On his return, in the month of October, he learns that Koller had just discovered, a little before Königstein, the analgesic power of this substance. He can therefore say to himself, quite rightly, that if he had not given free rein to his fantasy, if he had not given in to the insistent demands of a woman, he would have been the one "to pursue the matter further," and he would thus have secured for himself a discovery that would have borne his name. To the critics, as well as to his deepest wish, the dream responds that he is virtually the one who discovered cocaine. Likewise, he reminds us in this analysis, the dream is also a response to the reproach that his father used to direct at him when, at the age of seventeen, his passion for books got him into debt with the bookseller. The dream shows that his passion is not fruitless since his love of books has led him to write one. Here is how Freud sums up the argument for the defense: "'After all, I'm the man who wrote the valuable and memorable paper (on cocaine),' just as in the earlier dream I had said on my behalf: 'I'm a conscientious and hard-working student.' In both cases what I was insisting was: 'I may allow myself to do this'" (*SE* 4: 173; *GW* 2: 179).

The analysis of this dream leads us in fact far beyond the strict terms of the dream's latent "thoughts" into the determination of the unconscious desire, properly speaking, that mobilizes it. In chapter 7 of his book, Freud indicates that in order to recognize the source in unconscious desire through all the conscious or preconscious disguises one can rely on the fact that "in most dreams it is possible to detect a central point which is marked by peculiar sensory intensity," and this "central point is as a rule the direct representation of the wish-fulfilment" (*SE* 5: 561; *GW* 3: 567). He then refers us to section 2 of chapter 6 where, after having recalled how the essential elements played only a very minor role in the dream-thoughts, he teaches us to distinguish the apparent centering from the real centering of the dream: the dream is *differently "centered,"* its contents are organized around different elements than in the dream-thoughts. There appears here, in the very text of Freud, a new perspective emerging from the level of the latent dream-thoughts, which may be called *more formal than meaningful.*[6] Thus, he proposes as an example the dream of the botanical monograph, where the dream-thoughts turn around the difficulties, conflicts, and rivalries among colleagues, then around the idea that he "was in the habit of sacrificing too much for the sake of [his] hobbies," whereas the central point was "obviously the element 'botanical.'" This word is truly a crossroads where many associations of ideas meet up. We find ourselves in the middle of a workshop of ideas, in which, as for the weaver's masterpiece,

> a thousand threads one treadle throws,
> Where fly the shuttles hither and thither,
> Unseen the threads are knit together,
> And an infinite combination grows.[7]

Attached to the central word *botanical* are assorted elements of the previous day's experience: thus, the recollection of Professor Gärtner (Gardener in English) whom he had met when he was talking with Königstein. Gärtner was accompanied by his young wife, and Freud had complimented both of them on their *blooming* looks. In the same conversation, mention was made of two patients: one had the name *Flora*, the other was a patient to whom her husband had forgotten to bring *flowers* on her birthday. This "lady with the flowers" leads him to think, on the one hand, about the monograph on the cyclamen he had seen the day before in the window of a bookshop and, on the other, about the fact that the cyclamen is his wife's favorite flower. He reproaches himself on this score because he does not think often enough to offer them to her, whereas she, being "more generous than [he is]," never fails when she has the chance to bring him back from the market his *favorite flower*: an artichoke. We may note incidentally that this same expression, "favorite flower," figures in another dream from the same period, that of Count Thun. At the beginning of that dream, the count appeared and was "challenged to say something about the Germans, and declared with a contemptuous gesture that their *favourite flower* was colt's foot, and put some sort of dilapidated leaf—or rather the crumpled skeleton of a leaf—into his buttonhole" (*SE* 4: 209–10; *GW* 2: 215).

We will have occasion to return to this other favorite flower, which Freud, in the succeeding pages, will erroneously translate with the French flower name, *pissenlit* (*SE* 4: 213; *GW* 2: 219).

In addition, the word *botanical* recalls two other memories of his studies. One concerns his examination in botany at the university. It was a subject to which he had devoted little attention, with the result that when he had to identify a crucifer, he could not recognize it. The other memory is connected with the dried plant in the dream, "as though it had been taken from a herbarium." He is in secondary school and the headmaster calls together the older pupils and gives them the chore of cleaning a herbarium into which some little worms (*Bücherwürmer*) had found their way. The young Freud, however, was given only a few sheets to clean.

At the end of this *botanical chain*, Freud evokes what he calls a screen memory; it arises from the fragment "folded colour plate," which reminds him first of all of his liking for monographs when he was seventeen. He continues:

> There followed, I could not quite make out how, a recollection from very early youth. It had once amused my father to hand over a book with *coloured plates* (an account of a journey through Persia) for me and my eldest sister to destroy. Not easy to justify from the educational point of view! I had been five years old at the time and my sister not yet three; and the picture of the two of us blissfully pulling the book to pieces (leaf by leaf, like an *artichoke*, I found myself saying) was almost the only plastic memory I retained from that period of my life. Then, when I became a student, I had developed a passion for collecting and owning books, which was analogous to my liking for learning out of monographs: a *favourite hobby*. (The idea of "*favourite*" had already appeared in connection with cyclamens and artichokes.) I had become a *book-worm*. I had always, from the time I first began to think about myself, referred this first passion of mine back to the childhood memory I have mentioned. Or rather, I had recognized that the childhood scene was a "screen memory" for my later bibliophile propensities. (*SE* 4: 172–73; *GW* 2: 179)

At this point in the analysis, we can already see the outline of the profoundly intricate relation between book and woman, leaf and flower, picking (flowers) and eating. But we should not stop there in the exploration of the botanical vein, concerning which we now understand better why it is so closely joined to that other word *monograph*. "Not only the compound idea, 'botanical monograph,' however, but each of its components, 'botanical' and 'monograph' separately, led by numerous connecting paths deeper and deeper into the tangle of dream-thoughts" (*SE* 4: 282; *GW* 2: 289).

Although it would probably be incorrect to say that, by giving his five-year-old son a book to tear up, Jakob Freud was consciously offering him the possibility of carrying out his oedipal phantasm by means of substitution, nevertheless the way in which Sigmund relates this (screen) memory seems indeed to indicate what he made of this singular form of "reading": an extraordinarily satisfying defoliation and transgression. This is the point at which to wonder not so much about the generation gap that makes the newborn Sigmund already the uncle of his future playmates but rather about the singularity of the father Jakob's desire when he gives him a picture book to tear apart.[8] If it is a fact of experience that the unconscious speaks without regard to time, then one may find a repetition of the act of giving a book to his son in Jakob's gift of his own Bible to Sigmund for his thirty-fifth birthday. And one may also find a commentary on this gesture in the dedication that Jakob wrote for the occasion:

> My dear son,
>
> It was in the seventh year of your age that the spirit of God began to move you to learning. I would say the spirit of God speaketh to you: "Read in My book; there will be opened to thee sources of knowledge and of the intellect." It is the book of Books; it is the well that wise men have digged and from which lawgivers have drawn the waters of their knowledge.
>
> Thou hast seen in this Book the vision of the Almighty, thou hast heard willingly, thou hast done and hast tried to fly high upon the wings of the Holy Spirit. Since then I have preserved the same Bible. Now, on your thirty-fifth birthday I have brought it out from its retirement and I send it to you as a token of love from your old father.[9]

It is interesting in this regard to note that Freud, when he wonders about his fate, mentions willingly the flattering predictions of an old peasant woman when he was born (*SE* 4: 192; *GW* 2: 198) or that of the versifier in the Prater who promised the eleven- or twelve-year-old Sigmund a brilliant career, but he speaks little of what in this case might have been the mark of his father, which is all but confined to this incidental remark: "Not easy to justify [giving children a book to tear up] from the educational point of view!" The screen memory of the artichoke-book refers in fact, by means of a note (*SE* 4: 173; *GW* 2: 178), to the article from 1899 titled "Screen Memories." Now, we know, ever since S. Bernfeld established it in 1946, that the example at the center of this text is a thinly disguised autobiographical fragment.[10] This is to say that, at least in an "associative" sense, the oldest link in the botanical chain must be found here, which is in fact what becomes apparent. Here is the text:

> I see a rectangular, rather steeply sloping piece of meadow-land, green and thickly grown; in the green there are a great number of yellow flowers—evidently common dandelions. At the top end of the meadow there is a cottage and in front of the cottage door two women are standing chatting busily, a peasant-woman with a handkerchief on her head and a children's nurse [Nannie —s.l.]. Three children are playing in the grass. One of them is myself (between the age of two and three); the two others are my boy cousin [John, in fact his nephew — s.l.], who is a year older than me, and his sister [Pauline —s.l.], who is almost exactly the same age as I am. We are picking the yellow flowers and each of us is holding a bunch of flowers we have already picked. The little girl has the best bunch; and, as though by mutual agreement, we—the two boys—fall on her and snatch away her flowers. She runs up the meadow in tears and as a consolation the peasant-woman gives her a big piece of black bread. Hardly have we seen this than we throw the flowers away, hurry to the cottage and ask to be given some bread too. And we are in fact given some; the peasant-woman cuts the loaf with a long knife. In my memory the bread tastes quite delicious—and at that point the scene breaks off. (*SE* 3: 311; *GW* 1: 538)

This memory of flowers snatched or ripped away from Pauline probably marks one of the ultimate end points of Freud's analysis. It seems that we can identify there at least two or three of those crossroads that are, as we have been told, the points where unconscious desire burgeons above the surface.

Thus, it seems to us that, through these two screen memories, we must consider as major terms of the Freudian unconscious the words *reissen, entreissen* (tear, pull, rip, snatch), or their botanical variant, *pflücken*, to pick or pluck, on the one hand, and, on the other, the word *yellow, gelb.*

We'll begin by examining the paths that join up in the word *yellow.* There is first of all the path that is explicitly indicated by Freud and that leads from Gisela's yellow dress—already mentioned—to the screen memory itself. For, in the context of the analysis of the flowers torn from Pauline, we should recall Freud's evocations of his first love, when he was seventeen, for Gisela, the fifteen-year-old daughter of the Fluss family with whom he spent a vacation. It was the first time he had returned to Freiberg since the family's exodus when he was three. Right away he fell violently in love with Gisela but guarded the secret of his love jealously even though the separation following this brief idyll "brought [his] longings to a really high pitch" (*SE* 3: 313; *GW* 1: 540). It is true that the dress Gisela was wearing in his memory was a brownish yellow, just like, says Freud, certain flowers whose colors are lighter in the lowlands and darker at high altitudes.

By contrast, Freud says almost nothing of yellow as the color associated with Jews. He merely makes an allusion, in the analysis of the dream of Count Thun, to a botanical form of anti-Semitism, the war of the carnations that was then raging in Vienna: white carnations were the insignia of the anti-Semites, red carnations that of the social democrats.

From another angle, yellow, as every analyst of children knows, is the principal color of urethral eroticism, about which, moreover, Freud rather freely confides secrets concerning himself, identifying there the very source of his ambition, or even his megalomania, as he claims. There is nothing surprising for a francophone reader, therefore, in seeing the *pissenlit* get inscribed in the botanical series in a major way.[11] Obviously it is much more surprising for a German-speaking reader, for the name of the dandelion in German is *Löwenzahn*, which means literally "lion's tooth." It is at this point that we must review the analysis of the dream of Count Thun. When Freud comments on the count's assertion to the effect that the *favorite flower* of the Germans is colt's foot, *Huflattich*, he freely

associates on this word, which leads him into a series of associations with obscene and vulgar words both in German and in
French: from *Hund* [dog] to its French equivalent *chien*, from
chien . . . to *chier* [to shit]. Pulled along by the associative series of
the two excremental functions, he concludes with this remark:
"Moreover, I translated 'colt's foot'—whether rightly or wrongly I
could not tell—by the French 'pisse-en-lit'" (*SE* 4: 213; *GW* 2: 220).
Clearly, the translation is wrong according to the dictionary, for in
German a *pissenlit* is, as we've said, a *Löwenzahn*, lion's tooth.

We could likewise interrogate the dream of "the uncle with the
yellow beard" (*SE* 4: 137; *GW* 2: 143), where thoughts relating to
anti-Semitism come quickly to the surface. But we are going to
stop here with the yellow color of the "lion's teeth" because it will
lead us, via a trajectory that one can already guess thanks to the appearance of *teeth*, to the other major term: *ripping, tearing*. At the
beginning of the second section of chapter 5 of *The Interpretation
of Dreams*, where Freud intends to show that the sources of the
dream (unconscious desire) are to be found in childhood and right
before he again takes up the example of the botanical monograph,
he proposes an example supplied by a colleague "in his thirties."
This source is, I believe, the same as the one in the screen memory, that is, Freud himself.[12] Here is what this colleague told him:
He often dreamed of a *yellow lion* without finding any explanation
for this figure, until one day he discovered the exact same lion
from his dream in the form of a china ornament that had turned
up after a long disappearance.[13] His mother told him on this occasion that it had been his favorite toy as a child; he himself did
not remember this detail. The second story, attributed in the very
next lines to the "colleague of the yellow lion," seemed no less in-
structive to Freud.

> After reading Nansen's narrative of his polar expedition, he had a
> dream of being in a field of ice and of giving the gallant explorer gal-
> vanic treatment for an attack of sciatica from which he was suffering.
> In the course of analyzing the dream, he thought of a story dating
> from his childhood, which alone, incidentally, made the dream intel-
> ligible. One day, when he was a child of three or four, he had heard

the grown-ups talking of voyages of discovery and had asked his father whether that was a serious illness. He had evidently confused *Reisen* [voyages] with *Reissen* [gripes]. (*SE* 4: 191; *GW* 2: 196–97).

So we have returned to the second major word, *reissen* (tear, rip, snatch) or *pflücken* (pick, pluck). Let us note that if the confusion of *Reisen* with *Reissen* here is indeed, as one may assume, an element of Freud's autobiography, then his analysis must have helped somewhat to alleviate his phobia of traveling.

To pick, rip, tear, deflower: these seem to be the principal variants of the term *reissen*, a "perennial" element of the oldest level of memory. If we add to these some variations on the same word, we obtain the model of the possible confusions: *reisen* (to travel), *beissen* (to bite . . . into the delicious bread), *heissen* (to order, to name . . . to put one's name on some discovery).

Just as the Delft blue in the rebus dream of the "deux verres à la mer" could be legitimately taken as a formal indication to translate the figurative text into "painting by Vermeer," so too can one imagine that, for Freud, the representation of the newspaper *Fliegende Blätter* (literally, "flying pages") would tend to evoke by preference the "cabbage leaf," that is, the series book-artichoke rather than the series *verba volant* that it might also suggest.

To the question we are asking concerning criteria that permit one to prefer one interpretation of the rebus to another, the study of Freud's analysis of the dream of the botanical monograph leaves no doubt as to how to proceed. He writes:

> In most dreams it is possible to detect a central point which is marked by peculiar sensory intensity. . . . This central point is as a rule the direct representation of the wish-fulfilment, for, if we undo the displacements brought about by the dream-work, we find that the *psychical* intensity of the elements in the dream-thoughts has been replaced by the *sensory* intensity of the elements in the content of the actual dream. (*SE* 5: 561–62; *GW* 3: 567)

Freud then refers to the analysis of the botanical monograph dream and, as we have already emphasized, he insists that what really mat-

ter are not the themes of latent dream-thoughts (difficulties or rivalries among colleagues or the idea that he sacrifices too much for
the sake of his hobbies) but the *word botanical*. This word, which
is a part of the most manifest content, is *at the same time* the most
sensitive central core of the dream. As a veritable crossroad word
or keyword, a term of particular intensity, it figures, according to
Freud, the *direct fulfillment of the desire*. We will have to return to
the *formal* character of this identification of a term as central or
nodal, which is opposed, as we see, to an identification based on
the meaning or *the theme* of the dream's thoughts, even when they
are latent. "The dream is, as it were, differently centered" (*SE* 4:
305; *GW* 2: 310). We were thus able to see, through a true reading
of this analysis, the emergence of the crossroad words: *botanical*,
monograph, yellow, and finally the series *pick, rip, tear*.

     As we come to the end of this reading, we must get around to
what cannot be evaded indefinitely: the enigma of this wish fulfillment, *Wunscherfüllung*, which is *the realization of unconscious desire in the proper sense and the ultimate goal of analysis*. In the example that Freud proposes, his own, the terms of tearing away and revealing seem indeed to bring us closest to this, and the expression
"to reveal a secret" could be one of the unconscious models. This is
how what could be called one of Freud's fundamental phantasms
appears upon analysis, in its most stripped-down form. But it
would nevertheless be a misrecognition of its meaning to make of
it a more or less aggressive phantasm of deflowering. The fact that
Freud explicitly mentions this interpretation in his analysis of the
screen memory should not make us forget everything being said,
simultaneously, from the other side of the memory, the slice cut
from the loaf of bread with such a delicious taste. Suffice it to
point here to this other crossroad word constituted by the German
word for *loaf*, which is *Laib* and which to the ear is indistinguish-
able from the word *Leib*, body.
     What I would like to highlight is that the unconscious desire,
formalized by this phantasm, is not only an incestuous desire to
possess the mother, body, or breast and to take a delicious pleasure

in it, as suggested by the oral image of taking a big bite out of this fabulous bread, but, properly speaking, the desire to pluck (*pflücken*), to tear away (*ent-reissen*), to reveal (*enthüllen*), which is to say, desire for a desire reduced to its essential dimension, *for a movement that goes beyond, a desire almost freed from the fascination of the object.*

The experience of the defoliation of the mother-book given by the father certainly marks a turning point in Freud's history: there is no doubt that his "passion for books" is born at that moment. It is to this passion that he will turn, at seventeen, in order to forget his love for Gisela; it is this passion that he will invoke, unsuccessfully, when confronted by his father with his debt to the bookseller; it is this passion that will protect him, at nineteen, from his temptation to marry Pauline. But, and here is where one clearly sees all the difference, he will not be content to be a bibliophile, collector, and erudite reader of books. The book will not be frozen into a screen object, because Freud *will write* a book and he will write it on precisely the fact of desire. This book says that the unveiling of desire is accomplished in a transgression. This is how he fulfills his childhood desire, which may be expressed, following the model of his phantasm, as "tearing away" the secret from, in this case, dreams.

One can find hundreds of examples in Freud's work and life of this fundamental wish to transgress, in the literal sense of going beyond. Recall, first of all, the symptom of the impossible journey to the mother city of Rome, of his stopping, as did Hannibal, at the edge of Lake Trasimeno. This impossibility will persist until the book is done. Then, more literally, there is Freud's odd notion that sexual life was also the most elementary possibility at man's disposal for going beyond: "And after all," he writes in the conclusion of his analysis of the *non vixit* dream, "was not having children our only path to immortality?" (*SE* 5: 487; *GW* 3: 491). One senses, nevertheless, that this path, which Freud followed, did not really convince him. He says the same thing, and with more assurance, in his theoretical elaboration when he poses quite firmly the principle of the irreducibility of the sexual drives to any other biologi-

cal tendency: "sexuality is not to be put on a par with other functions of the individual; for its purposes go beyond the individual
and have as their content the production of new individuals."[14] It
is, however, only through his book that he really fulfills his wish.

One could certainly explain this fundamental requirement of
Freud's regarding the question of desire by interrogating, as he has
taught us to do, his relations with his mother. In fact, he took care
of this for us, with great lucidity, and we know through him that,
like one of his models, Goethe, he was a favorite son and loved by
the gods, which gave him his inexhaustible confidence and the in-
vincible energy that allowed him to go "to the very limits of the
human." This is no doubt a way of saying that he was gratified by
her very early; if one were persistent, one could probably find still
other echoes of that "delicious bread" that he most certainly tasted
and that leaves on those who have shared it a precious mark, which
is more indelible than a scar—even a scar inscribed behind the jaw,
as happened to Freud in punishment for a greediness that refused
to acknowledge any obstacles (*SE* 5: 560; *GW* 3: 566). As for the
degree of realization of this incestuous link to his mother, we can
recall not only the first memory of his mother *unveiling* her nudity
in front of him during a *journey* (*OP* 70) but also the only nightmare that he claims to remember, in which he sees his mother
dead, her face lit up with happiness, carried by three or four people
with birds' beaks (*SE* 5: 583; *GW* 3: 589). There is no doubt here:
the child Freud dreams that he is the cause not only of his mother's
death but also of her beatitude. Just as he had been gratified by her,
here he dreams that he gratifies her, not without making use, in
the circumstance, of the Book, the Philippson Bible (the one his
father will give him) to figure the "transport" of his mother via the
image of Egyptian gods with falcon heads he had seen represented
there.

This nightmare presents more clearly than any other dream the
enigma of wish fulfillment, the ultimate term aimed at in psychoanalysis. To be sure, the dream represents the mother as gratified, the very image of satisfaction. But the obvious meaning of
this figuration cannot suffice to guarantee a correct interpretation,

any more than the symbolism of the gesture "offering flowers to a woman" sufficed for the interpretation of the dream of the monograph.

In this case, it is the element of "people with birds' beaks" that, in Freud's expression, directly figures unconscious desire, just as the word *botanical* had done in the dream of the monograph. If one doubts even slightly the value of "people with birds' beaks" as figuration of the unconscious wish, one need only continue to follow Freud's reading carefully. One then remarks that, in the summary analysis of this nightmare, the bird with a curved beak whose head figures in the dream is called by Freud a "sparrowhawk" (*Sperber*). There is also the name Philippson, translator of the Bible in which Freud says he first saw the image of the Egyptian divinities. That name evokes the memory of an ill-mannered boy named Philippe, inasmuch as this rascal had revealed to him a vulgar term that in German can designate the sexual act: *vögeln* (from *Vogel*, bird). Since we know from elsewhere that Freud collected Egyptian antiquities, it may seem surprising that he speaks of a sparrowhawk when describing the head of the god Horus (who was represented, moreover, by a statuette in his collection), since it is usually described as the head of a falcon (*Falken*). Furthermore, the reader of Freud cannot forget here the quite amazing study from 1910, "Leonardo da Vinci and a Memory of His Childhood."

At the center of this latter essay, there is an autobiographical note of Leonardo's relating a veritable phantasm, which he claims to be a memory from earliest childhood: "I recall as one of my earliest memories that while I was in my cradle a vulture came down to me, and opened my mouth with its tail, and struck me many times with its tail against my lips."[15] Leonardo calls the bird in question a *nibbio*, that is, a kite. In German, a kite is a *Weihe* or a *Gabelweihe*, because of its long split tail [*Gabel*, fork]. Now, as Lacan has noted, Freud in fact translated *nibbio* with *Geier*, which is the German word for vulture, a much larger bird than the kite, which also differs from it by the form of its tail and the length of its neck.[16] One may impute Freud's error to a combination of effects: on the one hand, the effect of a repression of the series *Weihe*, which means "kite," but also "consecration," "sacredness," and is very close in sound to the series *Weib* (woman) and *Laib-Leib* (loaf-body) already mentioned, and, on the other hand, the effect of an attraction exerted by the series *Geier* (vulture, eagle), which approaches the sonority of the series *Geil* (concupiscent, lecherous).[17] Whatever the case may be, in the course of his analysis of the memory and with respect to the vulture introduced there in this way, Freud evokes the hieroglyph that had this form and that is supposed to have signified "mother" for the Egyptians. He also recalls on this occasion beliefs regarding the uniquely female sex of vultures, as well as the figuration of this maternal divinity endowed with an erect phallus. Eagle, sparrowhawk, vulture, or falcon: it seems in any case that the insistent element of this representation is indeed the nature of the bird's beak (and perhaps the diphthong), which always indicates for Freud the enigma of desire, whether in all its triviality (*vögeln, Geil*) or in its sacred character (*Weih*).

To grasp what psychoanalysis imposes on us, then, and as Freud never tires of saying, we still have to get rid of many prejudices. And especially here we must rid ourselves of two major habits: first, the way of considering the tension of desire on the model of the appeal to a need turned expectantly in the direction of an object that would be the proper one to gratify it. Obviously, psychoanalysis proposes no such thing, for *unconscious desire appears there as a formula*, surprising in its oddity, often absurd, a composite like the figure of an Egyptian god, literally like "botanical," "*reissen*," "people with birds' beaks." It is a formula, cipher, or letter that aims more at insisting, at repeating itself enigmatically than at saturating, gratifying, or suturing itself in some fashion.

The other prejudice that psychoanalysis leads us necessarily to renounce is, as already mentioned, the notion of the distinction between a deeply hidden and truthful reality, on the one hand, and a deceptive appearance, a directly accessible surface, on the other. To be sure, the didactic opposition between manifest and latent content allows for a limited interpretation, thereby sustaining this prejudice. Yet, notice how in the course of our reading *one and the same term* turns out in fact, upon analysis, to support the truth and its veiling: "people with birds' beaks," "yellow," "*reissen*," and "botanical" are just as much the concealment as the patent affirmation of the singularity of unconscious desire. Before coming back to it, we cannot insist too much here on this fact, which is coextensive with the whole possibility of psychoanalysis, namely: there is *no truth either before or beyond unconscious desire; the formula that constitutes it at the same time represents it and betrays it.* This is the very truth of unconscious desire, which is constantly reborn to reality by the perpetuation of transgression.

Finally, oddly enough, what appears at the end of an uncompromising analysis is unconscious desire itself as a formal construction and, as such, devoid of meaning but easily couched in a figure: "to snatch away yellow flowers" in its phantasmic composition, or "people with birds' beaks" in its hieroglyphic concision. We therefore find at the end of the analysis a formal composition analogous to that of the rebus with which we began. But this formal composition also turns out to be the very essence of the latent thoughts that nothing, or almost nothing, distinguishes from the manifest content, either in its terms or its organization. There could be no better illustration of the fact, crucial for analysis, that there is nothing beyond the text, or better yet, the letter.

§ 3 Taking the Body Literally, or How to Speak of the Body

One and the same text, or better yet one and the same letter, both constitutes and represents unconscious desire. In its ultimate aim, psychoanalysis thereby puts into question the common and convenient distinction between a term of reality and its representation. This may be surprising even to those most familiar with psychoanalysis.

Something in the absoluteness of this formulation seems to challenge Freud's point of view. Nothing is more evident, in fact, than Freud's very frequent invocation of the biological substratum opposed as such to the reflective nature of psychic representation. From this perspective, the psyche would seem to be the superstructure of a reality that is fundamentally organic. One could even wonder, therefore, how this position could be distinguished from what in psychiatry is called the organicist position, which is opposed to the psychogeneticist position and is imputed precisely to Freudians. Yet it is obvious that such a reading of Freud cannot reasonably be defended: whatever may be the insistence from one end to the other of his work on the fundamental character of the biological fact, this cannot be understood as a disavowal, still less a cancellation of the essence of his discovery. In fact, psychoanalysis exists in reality and develops only at the level of representations. To illustrate this fact, one need but recall that repression, which is the keystone of the psychic apparatus,[1] operates only on elements of representation, to the exclusion of any other reality of the drives, which has no place in psychic life. The unconscious is constituted by primitively repressed representations,[2] which are at the origin of the offshoots that themselves fall under the force of repression in the strict sense, thereby constituting the manifestly active core of the psychic apparatus. Thus, according to the inventor of psychoanalysis, there is no possible doubt: the reality of psychic life, the truth that is the unconscious and that confronts us, is composed of representative elements of the drive (figurative representations or affective charges): "An instinct [*Trieb*] can never become an object of consciousness—only the idea that represents the instinct can. Even in the unconscious, moreover, an instinct cannot be represented otherwise than by an idea. If the instinct did not attach itself to an idea or manifest itself as an affective state, we would know nothing about it."[3] As we know, the work of analysis consists in making possible some access to this unconscious order of "repressed" representations so as to reestablish their logic and discover their singular coherence in each case.

It is certainly not easy, however, to remain at this truly logical level of unconscious desire, which is why, when one encounters a difficulty in the deciphering work that makes for the originality of psychoanalysis, one naturally has recourse to more traditional, but also in a sense more regressive, ways of thinking. There is some comfort to be found in the substitution of the biological model with its metaphoric opacity for the logical order of representations that psychoanalysis promotes. The drive is thereby held to be an organic fact, as, for example, when Freud invokes it in the form of movements of the drive (*Triebregungen*) or, even more simply, when he describes it as an impulse that has a "biological nature."[4] According to his own definition, however, the drive should be taken as a "concept on the frontier between the mental and the somatic" or even, as he adds in the same sentence, "as the psychical representative of the stimuli originating from within the organism and reaching the mind, as a measure of the demand made upon the mind for work in consequence of its connection with the body."[5] Finally, if one recalls the vital point of the psychoanalytic perspective, namely, that the drive strictly speaking cannot have any other existence except in its representatives, the ambiguity of the Freudian position becomes manifest in all its scope and may be summed up very well in this sentence: "The nucleus of the unconscious consists of instinctual representatives which seek to discharge their cathexis; that is to say, it consists of wishful impulses [*Wunschregungen*]. These instinctual impulses [*Triebregungen*] are co-ordinate with one another."[6]

In this fragment, Freud refers simultaneously to the "representative," which is an eminently logical or "logifiable" term, and to "instinctual impulses" (confused moreover with the wishful impulses), which latter notion implies in fact the primacy of a biological reality.[7] Looking at the problem in this way, one is confronted with two apparently contradictory points of view: On the one hand, there is the notion that everything in the psychoanalytic field is situated at the level of representations conceived of as formal elements. On the other hand, there is the notion that the essence of the unconscious process should be situated at the level of impulses of the instincts or drives, that is, of an energy that has an organic nature. But it is quite clear that when the debate is initiated in this way, and no matter what the intention may be, one goes against Freudian thinking by underscoring an opposition of "psychic" and "organic" terms, whereas the difficult concept of the drive, which constitutes Freud's true contribution, tends to comprehend precisely this dualism within a truly novel dynamism. The originality of this concept, described as a limit, is that it grounds the unconscious outside the categories of the biological and the psychological understood in their pre-Freudian senses. In other words, the division or gap grounding the dimension of representation in the whole doctrine of the drives is without question situated elsewhere and otherwise than in the traditional opposition between the soul and the body. This is what we will show in the most demonstrative fashion by analyzing a major libidinal position, that of perversion.

In the case of perversion, the object of desire appears in its paradoxical reality. That woman is man's object of desire raises no questions—although it should[8]—because in general one is careful not to question the objective singularity of an attribute or the impalpable odor of essential femininity. But that a man could be the object for a man or, better yet, that a shoe or a piece of lingerie could polarize desire, this sets off a series of questions. The preferred fetish object is, as we know, something altogether ordinary and in common use, which is not distinguished a priori by its erotic value. For those, and they are the majority, who have not themselves chosen it as fetish, the object would be distinguished rather by a taint of vulgarity (for example, panties) or by the somewhat ridiculous character it has when isolated (for example, a boot that is a little out of fashion) or yet again by a certain hint of repulsiveness as may be produced, for example, by an orthopedic accessory. In any case, one cannot say that the fetish object is in itself altogether indifferent: fur or whips, iron or rubber, are deemed neutral only by those who give in or pretend to give in to the effects of a more or less shared repression. But, let us repeat, if one can easily conceive how, for man, this or that curve of the feminine body is able to excite the movement or desire and set off the organic process that manifests it, one needs some more time for reflection to conceive how a piece of fluff or rubber—presuming, of course, that its fetishistic properties have been selected only by another—can set off in this other, in the most vivid and ineluctable manner, the cycle of desire culminating in orgasm. To be sure, one soon realizes that it is possible, through a series of associations proceeding by way of contiguity, to reconstitute the chain leading from the fetish object back to the body and more precisely to the sexual parts.

We know the explanation Freud gives, based on his analyses, for the value of the fetish object: it is the substitute for the penis that the little boy, at a very young age, attributed to his mother and to every woman.

> In all cases the meaning and purpose of the fetish turned out, in analysis, to be the same. It revealed itself so naturally and seemed to me so compelling that I am prepared to expect the same solution in all cases of fetishism. When now I announce that the fetish is a substitute for the penis, I shall certainly create disappointment; so I has-

ten to add that it is not a substitute for any chance penis, but for a particular and quite special penis that had been extremely important in early childhood but had later been lost. That is to say, it should normally have been given up, but the purpose of the fetish is precisely designed to preserve it from extinction. To put it more plainly: the fetish is a substitute for the woman's (the mother's) phallus that the little boy once believed in and—for reasons familiar to us—does not wish to give up.[9]

This explanation has been shown, in all analyses of perversion, to be profoundly correct.

Without question, the fetish constitutes the most demonstrative example of the mechanism of perverse desire and perhaps even a model for the doubled features of the cycle of any desire. In fact, since Freud, we also know how much this analysis of the perverse position has attenuated the opposition between normal sexuality and its aberrations. The autonomous activity of the "erotogenic zones"—and any part of the body can constitute an erotogenic zone, as we will make clear later—illustrates the play of the partial drives that characterizes infantile sexual activity in its "polymorphous perversity." And it is the same partial drives that are at work in the practice of a "normal" adult sexual life.

> In view of what was now seen to be the wide dissemination of tendencies to perversion we were driven to the conclusion that a disposition to perversions is an original and universal disposition of the human sexual instinct and that normal sexual behaviour is developed out of it as a result of organic changes and psychical inhibitions occurring in the course of maturation. . . . The perversions were thus seen to be on the one hand inhibitions, and on the other hand dissociations, of normal development. Both these aspects were brought together in the supposition that the sexual instinct of adults arises from a combination of impulses of childhood into a unity, an impulsion with a single aim.[10]

We have dwelled on the strangeness of the fetish object because, we said, it makes the dimension of desire appear in the full scope of its paradoxical reality. If one follows step by step the singular chain that culminates in the choice of substitutive object, one finds at the origin in every case a single term, the same term: *the penis of the mother*. To be sure, the term is surprising as the ultimate reference, for it is difficult to imagine a more "unthinkable," a more naturally unreal, term. Objectively, the penis of the mother does not exist, and its nature consists in the representation of a wish on the part of the child, a kind of false hypothesis that is necessary for his logic. Psychoanalysts are probably not the only ones who know how often in dreams one comes upon some special (or anonymous) woman supplied with a phallus. Thus, we find as the focal point of perverse desire a figurative term, *penis of the woman*, whose proper nature doubtless resides in the contradiction it harbors, in all its absurdity, and also in its function as mark or mask of the lack that it underscores by denying or recognizes by disavowing.

It is worthwhile, at this point, to recall that when Freud attempts to define the movement he calls desire or wish (*Wunsch*), he evokes the mnemic image of a perception (*Erinnerungsgbild einer Wahrnehmung*), whose cathexis (*Besetzung*) reactualizes the perception and constitutes the realization of the desire. Thus, for example, thanks to the excitation produced by the actualization of a basic need such as thirst, the recathected memory of the act of drinking that quenches thirst would cause to reappear the perception of milk or water so as to fulfill the wish.[11]

We see that the object that puts the wish in play is radically distinguished from the object that supplies the satisfaction of a need. Whereas the object of need may easily be conceived on the model of salt that allows the rechloridation of a dehydrated organism, or of sugar that puts an end to hypoglycemic coma, the object of desire must be conceived in an altogether different manner.

Freudian analysis of the value of the fetish in perverse desire brings to the fore the *penis of the woman*, which stands for the object of a wish or a phantasm that the child has been unable to give up. The object of perverse desire is, then, indeed a dreamed-of, fantasized, or we might say hallucinated term. In more general terms, as we have just read in Freud, the object that excites in all cases the movement called desire is a hallucinated object or, more exactly, the cathexis or recathexis of a "mnemic image."

One may thus say that this animating function of desire is carried out by what is basically a paradoxical term, a hallucinated object. This crucially important term—about which for the moment we cannot say whether it is flesh or word, object or letter—requires that we question in a new way the concept of body since the dimension of pleasure (*Lust*), around which the very possibility of the desire in question is organized, cannot be conceived of except in a body.

Before getting to this question of the corporeal nature of the object, which is the cause of desire, and in order to take up the question raised at the beginning of this chapter, we may remark, finally, that the division presupposed by the concept of representation would not be situated in psychoanalysis between, on the one hand, an objective reality and, on the other, its figuration in a meaning. Rather, it is situated between, on the one side, a hallucinated reality, which is the mnemic image of a lost gratifying object, and, on the other, a substitute object, which may be a "formula-object" like the one that constitutes phantasms or an instrumental whatnot, such as a fetish. One could even envision situating the division of representation in a still more radical way, between the presence of the hallucinated reality and the absence of the object of satisfaction, between the memory of the lost one-and-only-one and the attempt to find it again in a repeated staging.

We have seen, therefore, that the organizing and, no doubt, triggering element of the movement of desire (*Wunsch*) is basically identified by Freud as a term that escapes any simple grasp, an imaginary object at the very least. But after having likewise insisted on the illusory character of the object, we ought nevertheless to recall in no uncertain terms one obvious thing: the satisfaction implied by the cycle of desire, whether one calls it pleasure or *jouissance*, cannot be fulfilled (or conceived of) except in a body.

But which body?

That which is designated by the name body in physiological

anatomy cannot accommodate, in its descriptive illustrations or in the metabolism of basic needs, either the phantom organ that is the penis of the woman or the hallucinated object that is the lost breast. A more specifically determined body is in question in psychoanalysis. Which one? A "whole body [as] an erotogenic zone," as Freud wrote in 1938.[12]

The notion of erotogenic zone, which appears very early in Freud's writings (*OP* 52 [Dec. 6, 1896]), designates an area of the body that is capable of becoming the center of an *excitation of a sexual type* and, principally, the portals of the body through which occur the exchanges of the organism under the sign of the most intensely pleasurable or unpleasant emotion and sensations. After having considered as possibly erotogenic only the whole of the outer covering—skin, mucous membranes, and orifices—Freud extends this possibility in the course of an investigation of hypochondria.[13] He extends, that is, the possibility of being a center of sexual-type excitation to all organs figured within the body, a possibility that the psychosomatic field endeavors to explore with some pertinence. Definitively, then, one can say that any part of the body can become erotogenic or, turning the proposition around, that the entire body can be said to be erotogenic. Nevertheless, in the axis of the Freudian concept of the erotogenic zone it would in fact seem preferable to say in a more precisely articulated fashion that *the body is a set of erotogenic zones*.

This notion of erotogenic zone, however, takes on its full meaning only when one correctly defines the excitation or the excitability of a *sexual* type that characterizes it. Despite the very wide reception of psychoanalysis today, we know to what extent there in fact persists a misunderstanding about sexuality in its strictly psychoanalytic sense. It is difficult, however much one may try, to fend off the idea that the sexual game ought to unfold according to the simple rules of a natural complementarity and a reproductive aim and that it is a matter finally—as Freud says moreover[14]—of a basic physiological need that ought to have a specific object fit to satisfy it. Opposed to this teleological perspective, the emphasis in psychoanalysis is placed, by the same Freud of course, on the fact of pleasure, which cannot in any way be reduced to the simple exercise of the organic function. Jean Laplanche and Jean-Baptiste Pontalis, in the wake of Lacan, put it this way in their *The Language of Psycho-analysis*: "The fulfillment of unconscious wishes is a response to very different requirements, and functions according to very different laws, from the satisfaction of the vital needs."[15] If this is so, then the problem psychoanalysis has put forward in a novel way is finally posed as follows: *what about sexual pleasure?* For the moment, we cannot answer that question but only situate it as well as possible.

In the framework of the energetic metaphor to which Freud readily resorts, pleasure is identified as the sensation that marks the end of a state of tension, which is aptly represented by the state of erection.[16] What the recourse to this metaphor makes clear is that the time of pleasure, or *jouissance*, is this time of difference, in this case the difference between more and less tension, a difference that is itself ungraspable, the quick of desire, a difference that is not the measure but the grounds of the possibility of measure.

Excitation or excitability of the sexual type, which specifies the erotogenic zone and which we are attempting to characterize, would thus be defined as the capacity of an area of the body to be the center of an immediately accessible, felt difference—pleasure or unpleasure—and to register in some way the mark of that difference. Here, the body indeed appears as it does in phantasms or delusions, that is, as the great book on which is inscribed the possibility of pleasure and in which is hidden "the impossible knowledge concerning sex."[17]

An erotogenic zone, therefore, seems to be defined as an area of the body where the fade-out or syncope of a difference stays marked and, still more precisely, where the terms between which the interval of pleasure opens up—lips of a mouth, lids of an eye, the exquisitely different and sensitive point of an epidermis in some secret border—can come together again. The excitation or excitability of the zone may be conceived of as the appeal constituted by the rift, opened and marked in this way, for the impossible return of the same pleasure. It is this difference frozen in its irreducible interval that is the very essence of the sexual drive in the Freudian sense. What is thereby marked or inscribed in the body can be considered just as well a point of appeal, a calling point, as a focus of energy. And that to which Freud gives the name "partial drive," on the basis of partially specified zones, are what come to be organized under the primacy of the genital zone. But here we must observe that this genital primacy, from the psychoanalytic perspective, does not arise from the importance of the genitalia's reproductive function. On the contrary, it arises from the privilege of this zone in the order of the inscription of or search for that difference in sensation that is pleasure. This zone is the chosen ground for the extreme modifications in which the very notion of organ is subverted because the function and its aim disappear into the order of *jouissance*, as I will make clear in a more detailed manner in a later chapter.

It is very tempting, and indeed it commonly happens, to confuse the fact of pleasure with the good functioning of the organ, even though we know that in the economy of its own order this functioning ought to be perfectly silent: the drowsy euphoria of digestion or, on the contrary, its anguishing torments constitute already a disorder of good gastric functioning, which may be either pleasant or unpleasant. In fact, the pleasure machine we were evoking a moment ago not only does not coincide with the organic apparatus, but, as we shall see, it even seems to be basically opposed to that apparatus. To produce pleasure, in sum, something like a perceptible rift must appear; an interval, a difference, a nothing has to open up that can, for the space of an instant, offer an empty reflection of the absolute of *jouissance*, a moment in which tension is annulled or, better yet, in which the terms that maintain the interval of difference are effaced. In that moment, which is the moment of pleasure, difference seems to annul itself in the illusion of a "pure difference."[18] From another point of view, this moment can also be described as a syncopation or countertempo in the sense in which, in well-written music, the beat sometimes can and must fall, in a latent or manifest way, on the interval between the represented or representable beats of the measure.

What must be emphasized is that the order of pleasure really is inscribed in counterpoint to the organic order and as such, because of the beat that falls on the interval between the elements of the system, it constitutes strictly speaking the subversion of that system. That avatars of a pleasure of the mouth can, in extreme cases, lead to a fatal undernutrition perfectly illustrates this latent antinomy, which manifests itself in part in anorexia as well as in the excesses of alcoholism. One could say that just as the organic order tends to reduce the tensions of differences according to a program of ideal homeostasis, so the order of pleasure tends to valorize the sensible interval by which this same-and-other-body opens onto the absolute of *jouissance*. The privilege of the genital zone, to which we will have to return,[19] derives from the fact that it seems to be both the instrument of an organic function of reproduction and the key piece in a pleasure machine. On this latter score—as keystone of an erotogenic body—the genital zone is thus agent and witness of the subversion of the organic order.

To arrive at a clear conception of this essential notion of erotogenic zone, it remains for us now to describe the singularity of the inscription in the body. Terms such as *mark* or *fixation* are used necessarily to describe the installation and especially the almost ineradicable persistence of erotogeneity in a point of the body. As we said, any region whatever of the body can become the center of a sexual-type excitability, which can be verified by the great variety of clinical histories. But what is it in any singular history that privileges one zone rather than another, that establishes in some sense a hierarchy of erotogenic investments, and that singularizes genital primacy? We said that the portals of the body, given their function of exchange, are offered in a preferential and virtually necessary fashion to erotogenization. But merely to underscore in this way the predisposition found in the givens of anatomophysiology is not enough to isolate the fact of a fixation. At most, it focuses our attention on the apparatus that allows erotogeneity to be installed in a zone. The process can be simply (albeit incompletely) described with respect to one of the predisposed zones. An appropriate object comes to appease the tension of a physiological need that the organ manifests; there results a satisfaction that, in a reverse manner from the appeasement provided by the chosen object of which no trace will remain, is inscribed like the expectation of or call for the return of an impossible "same." Thus, the breast or the bottle comes to appease the hunger-thirst of the infant, but what remains is the trace of satisfaction that will persist as a call, even before hunger recurs, and that will from now on be added as distinct expectation to the renewed demand of the need.

We saw that pleasure, in the sexual sense of the term, is born from a play within the memory of satisfaction. It is clear, therefore, that this pleasure is distinct and different in its principle from the appeasement of physiological need. But for a satisfaction to be inscribed, in a clear-cut manner, as focus of a call without response, a supplementary factor is necessary: the appeasement must already be regarded as *jouissance* in the eyes of another, the one who in this case gives nourishment. The inscription in the body happens when this sexual value is projected by another onto the place of satisfaction. It is in this projection of desire, which supposes the eye or the breast to be already themselves marked with erotogeneity, that the truth of the relation between two bodies is to be situated, a truth that here clearly manifests itself as sexual in its nature.

The process of erotogenization allows for, curiously enough, a more rigorous description if one takes into consideration the linked moments that lead up to the "opening" or the "inscription" of an erotogenic zone in a point of the integument. To be sure, one can consider that the surface of the skin, like a limit representing the inverse equivalent of the edge of an orifice, "needs" the caress of another skin. But this is not the aspect we mean to accentuate here. Let us imagine rather the softness of a mother's finger playing "innocently," as during lovemaking, with the exquisite dimple next to the baby's neck and the baby's face lighting up in a smile. We can say that the finger, with its loving caress, imprints a mark in this hollow, opens a crater of *jouissance*, inscribes a letter that seems to fix the indiscernible immediacy of the illumination. In the hollow of the dimple, an erotogenic zone is opened, an interval is fixated that nothing will be able to erase. This is where the play of pleasure will be produced in an elective manner provided an object, any object, comes along to revive in this place the brilliance of the smile fixed by the letter.

In this example, we can see more clearly that what makes the erotogenic inscription possible is the fact that the caressing finger is itself, for the mother, an erotogenic zone. This finger, in its essential libidinal value, can be called a "letter-holder" or inscriber to the extent that, as an erotogenic zone of the mother, a letter fixes into its flesh the interval of an exquisite difference. With this last example, the "projection of desire," which we were evoking a moment ago in an approximate fashion, can be analyzed easily.

As we have just seen, the effect of this projection, like an impact on a targeted body, is the opening or the "creation" of an erotogenic zone. This is to say that the erotogenic zone, whether we are talking about the erotogenization of an orifice or of a point of the integument, can be defined as a place of the body where access to "pure difference" (the experience of pleasure) produced there remains marked by a distinctive trait, a letter. Of this letter one can say either that it is inscribed in this place or that it is posed in its abstraction from the body. We will see in a moment how the letter understood in this manner constitutes at once the limit of and the access to *jouissance*.

For now, let us do no more than underscore the fact that *this definition of the erotogenic zone pivots around the immediacy of access to the "pure difference" that it stigmatizes.* Since one must remark that, outside of this approach, any reference to "pure difference" is necessarily mediated and, for that reason, is an effacement or annulment of difference as such, we understand the extraordinary privilege that remains marked as erotogeneity. The Freudian definition of the erotogenic zone as an area of a sexual-type excitation or excitability corresponds to a descriptive mode of the same privilege, in which sex is taken as the name of difference.

One can say metaphorically that an interval is fixed in the place in which difference was produced and that the play of desire will be able to unfold around this encircled lack, according to the rule of its illusions. There is above all the retrospective illusion of a lost first object, inducing a state of lack wherein the movement of desire is originated. As we have just seen, this is an illusion inasmuch as the agent of the opening is not an object that hides or closes the gap but a letter that imprints or fixes it. Nonetheless, the objectality of the caressing finger, even in this "first" occurrence, cannot be disputed, except to say that it is not this objectality that constitutes the "first" lack but indeed the letter made by the erotogenic finger.[20] The object, as such, is what then manifests itself, "in the place" of this *lost letter*;[21] its effect, in this erotogenic field, is to revive the feeling of difference, to recall the syncope of pleasure.

For the lost letter, then, an indifferent object has been substituted, in fact any object whatsoever, which is qualified to recall pleasure only by its value as object.

It is true that in a second moment the cycle of repetitions culminates in the choice of a determined object, which is a substitute for as well as a stranger to the first letter. To replace the mythical lost first breast, anything whatsoever that one puts in the mouth can do the trick, up until the day when the choice settles on the ear of a stuffed monkey, which becomes once again—sometimes for a long period—the obligatory mediator of all appeasements.[22]

That any object whatsoever can, in principle, fulfill this role in the play of pleasure may be surprising, even when we read the following assertion in Freud: "[The object] is what is most variable about an instinct [*Trieb*] and is not originally connected with it but becomes assigned to it only in consequence of being particularly fitted to make satisfaction possible. . . . It may be changed any number of times in the course of the vicissitudes which the instinct undergoes during its existence."[23] We must pause over this paradox in order to grasp that it is not some particular determination of the object that is in play in the cycle of desire but rather *its very quality as object*. A new question arises here: what is an object in the economy of pleasure? We will attempt to reply in the next chapter, but for the moment we will do no more than sketch the outline of a possible response.

Just as the letter has now been situated in its psychoanalytic sense as a trait that constitutes and marks in a place on the body the surfacing of *jouissance* in the immediacy of an exquisite difference, so too the object, in the economy of the unconscious, must first be identified by the function it fulfills relative to the stigmata constituted by the erotogenic zone. From this perspective we can say that, contrary to the letter that seems to fixate difference (which is, nonetheless, irreducible in its nature), the object tends to hide it or efface it. The object masks indiscernible difference; it presents itself as real, an objectal "nothing" suitable to zero, "indivisible [*insécable*]" (Lacan), and perfectly detached.[24] It is that some "thing," *res*, or little nothing whose insignificance corresponds, in its opacity, to the essential difference that it is intended to conceal.[25]

Hence, there is nothing surprising in the fact that the object, in the ordinary sense, designates the reality-term that is the individual in his or her density and (relative) organic coherence, inasmuch as the "noises of life" cover over his or her animating death. But what is important to grasp here is that this physical body, in its surface and its density, is offered to or resists, in any case supports, the erotogenic inscription-incision just as the page in a book sustains, causes to appear, and in a sense constitutes the letter inscribed there.

On the basis of this elucidation of the notion of erotogeneity, we can foresee the profoundly intricate relation of the letter and the object, which we will therefore call their *intrication*. We will have occasion to return to this in several ways.

The body in question in psychoanalysis must be conceived of, we said following Freud, as a set of erotogenic zones. This is moreover how it is represented in the dreamlike constructions of surrealism, where one finds odd assemblages of a hand and a mouth, eyes and fingers, jaws and backs, or yet again the brain and the belly.

A questioning of this notion of erotogenic zone, however, essentially brings to light its contradictory dimension as the place of an atopia. On the one hand, "pure difference" or annulment is identified by the unique privilege of immediate access constituted by the fact of *jouissance*, in which every topical reference is effaced. But, on the other hand, something remains in a place on the body, as limit and (measured) access to *that empty focus where the lack of a letter has been assured, or revealed, for each and everyone.*

One sees outlined, then, in proportion to the insistence of the erotogenic fact, both the letter and the object: the former as function of fixation, the latter as function of concealment.

Thus conceived, the letter (to speak provisionally only of the letter, excluding the psychoanalytic concepts of object and subject) *cannot be detached from its essential erotogenic value.* One must observe that this use of the term *letter*, which is imperative for the psychoanalyst, does not at all correspond to the commonly understood use. But the distance separating common usage from this strict sense (the correct sense, in my opinion, when speaking of the unconscious) can easily be acknowledged. One need only consider (as we will have ample occasion to in Chapter 6) that the trait of the letter is "originarily" drawn as a bar that fixates and annuls *jouissance*. It suffices then to let oneself be carried along by this essentially *repressive* function of the letter in order, at the other end of the trajectory, to take it as a term "pure" of any sexual implication.

To take the body literally is, in sum, to learn to spell out the orthography of the name composed by the erotogenic zones that constitute it. It is to recognize in each letter the singularity of the pleasure (or the pain) that that letter fixates, and to identify by the same token the series of objects in play.

§ 4 The Body of the Letter, or the Intrication of the Object and the Letter

Any object whatsoever can, in principle, trigger the movement of desire: the curve of a shoulder as well as a piece of rubber, a person's hair or foot, the other sex. But also, depending on the body, the same sex can evoke pleasure. Faced with this observation, which clinical experience forces us to accept despite all appearances to the contrary, one has to admit that the very quality of object is put fundamentally in question by what sets pleasure in play.

The object in question here is the term around which the cycle of desire develops, and for the moment at least it can be defined only in function of the erotogenic zone, that major constitutive element of the body of pleasure. This is what we sketched out previously when we referred to its function as the concealment of the erotogenic interval.[1]

Necessarily different from the difference it revives as zonal pleasure, the object must be conceived of as foreign to the body it excites. In this notion of foreignness, we ought not to overlook, in passing, the true origin of the phantasm of complementarity with which the question of desire is commonly closed down. For it is true that the representation of a gaping mouth filled by the breast ordinarily suffices to satisfy any attempt at thinking. The object is fundamentally the other body, and the encounter with it actualizes or makes perceptible the essential dimension of separation. While the erotogenic zone can be conceived of as the limit that encircles perceptible difference in its essential irreducibility, the object constitutes the term of a measurable separation that, in a certain way, is reducible even up to the cancellation of the encounter. Whereas the interval that makes for the perceptible difference of two lips can never be reduced, still less effaced, the interval separating the mouth from the object that will appease its desire can, by contrast, be reduced to the point of the cancellation of any distance.

It seems that the object can indeed be characterized by its quality of being separate, inasmuch as the interval of this separation makes manifest at the same time the dimension of the space and the possible annulment of the interval inscribed there. But this separation of the between-two-bodies, in which is revealed the primordial model of alterity, is not enough to account for the fact that the object appears, in practice, not only as another body, in its coherence or its organic unity, but much more often as a piece that is in its turn detached or fallen away from the whole.[2] Thus, the breast (to again take up this suggestive example), contrary to obvious anatomy, is found to be literally detached from the whole of the maternal body by the nursing infant who eats his or her fill of it: it is as if the division of the separation between-two-bodies were projected onto the limits of the object that supplies the satisfaction of the drive issuing from the oral erotogenic zone. And, consequently, just like any lollipop or pacifier, the breast is detached, and, as such, it is by the same token qualified as an object around which the circuit of oral pleasure will be able to pivot and find satisfaction.

Hence, just as any part of the body may be an erotogenic zone and thus potentially a "letter," so too any part of the body can become an object. However, whereas the bodily zone, in order to assume the function of a letter, must fixate or limit a perceptible and fundamentally irreducible difference—which is in a way intrinsic—the same point of the body, in order to assume the function of object, must distinguish itself from the whole through an extrinsic difference, which is analogous to the interval of distance in the between-two-bodies. We have seen with the example of the breast that the separation of the object is not necessarily the result of a real cut but essentially, as Lacan has shown, the result of a division.[3] This division separates the object from the erotogenic whole so as to make of it a term that then becomes, for the duration of its exclusion, inert and "indivisible" [*insécable*], out of reach of any new perceptible difference such as the erotogenic difference that gets inscribed on the body.

Two types of quite different intervals, then, come into play in the economy of pleasure: on the one hand, the interval that marks the separation of the object from the body (a variant of the between-two-bodies); on the other hand, the interval of the perceptible difference that is capable of inscription on the body as erotogenic zone.

In being thus distinguished or "differentiated" by a sort of extrinsic division, the object seems to become the tangible representative, one could say the positive complement, of the irreducible intrinsic difference that is set within the limits of the erotogenic zone. By the indivisibility it presents, in its derivative forms, to a conceptual or concrete manipulation, the object maintains a privileged relation with the indiscernible difference that makes for the exquisite sensitivity of the erotogenic zone. This relation between the letter and the object, which cannot be univocally described, appears as the model of the one that constitutes the sexual relation properly speaking.[4]

We see here in outline the definition of the objectal quality. Its function in libidinal economy, as a sort of *indifferent* pivot around which is reflected the cycle of desire (or more exactly the circuit of the drive),[5] accentuates at the same time the intrinsic neutrality (indifference) of the object and, correlatively, its determination by a kind of "extrinsic" division. One may thus say that the object, as part (a separate piece) of the body, *represents*, in the ordinary sense of the term, the dimension of essential alterity implicated in the conception of the erotogenic body. Whereas an organization of erotogenic zones, like a set of letters, maintains itself only through a fundamental alterity in relation to a missing term (as we will explain in detail later),[6] the object comes "in the place" of the lost letter and therefore represents alterity or foreignness in an immediate fashion.

Moreover, this question about the quality that belongs properly to the object brings out the profound intrication of the literal function and the objectal function. It does so insofar as the object is defined as that which comes in the place of the lost letter. Or, inversely, one could say that the object, in its opacity, takes the place of certainty concerning this lack.

To be sure, it remains no less difficult to understand this play around the immediacy of annulment achieved by pleasure. To say that the letter fixates difference and that the object seems to guarantee difference by concealing it may seem, to some, a long way from the problems posed by the practice of psychoanalysis.

Therefore, we are going to try now, through a more clinical approach, to bring out how the object and the letter function in the course of an analysis. In passing, we will see that this procedure necessarily makes manifest, in the unfolding of those intermediate formations between the conscious and the unconscious we call phantasms, dreams, and symptoms, the derivative or secondary level that is, properly speaking, the level of clinical procedure.

When, in his attempted analysis of the Wolf Man, Freud had brought to light the "scene with Grusha," he considered that "the problem of the treatment had every appearance of having been solved" (*SE* 17: 94; *GW* 12: 128). Indeed, with this scene he had found an event that the patient really remembered "without any conjectures or intervention on [Freud's] part" and that presented itself as a first identifiable effect of the supposed primal scene, one could almost say as proof that his hypothesis was correct.

Let us look in detail at the discovery and the content of this scene with Grusha. Freud and his patient had been busy considering once again the still-enigmatic memory of one of his childhood symptoms, from the same period as his fear of wolves: the butterfly phobia. "Once he was running after a beautiful big butterfly, with striped yellow wings which ended in points, in the hope of catching it. (It was no doubt a 'swallow-tail.') He was suddenly seized with a terrible fear of the creature, and, screaming, he gave up the chase" (*SE* 17: 16; *GW* 12: 39).

Despite repeated attempts, the butterfly—called *Babotchka* in Russian, which is similar to *Babouchka*, little grandmother—did not give up its secret, until one day "there emerged, timidly and indistinctly, a kind of recollection":

> at a very early age, even before the time of the nurse, he must have had a nursery-maid who was very fond of him. Her name had been the same as his mother's. He had no doubt returned her affection. It was, in fact, a first love that had faded into oblivion. But we agreed that something must have occurred at that time that became of importance later on.
>
> Then on another occasion he emended this recollection. She could not have had the same name as his mother; that had been a mistake on his part, and it showed, of course, that in his memory she had become fused with his mother. Her real name, he went on, had occurred to him in a roundabout way. He had suddenly thought of a store-room, on the first estate, in which fruit was kept after it had been picked, and of a particular sort of pear with a most delicious taste—a big pear with yellow stripes on its skin. The word for "pear" in his language was "*grusha*," and that had also been the name of the nursery-maid.

Freud concludes: "It thus became clear that behind the screen-memory of the hunted butterfly the memory of the nursery-maid lay concealed." Finally, the memory emerges: "Very soon after this there came the recollection of a scene, incomplete, but so far as it was preserved, definite. Grusha was kneeling on the floor, and beside her a pail and a short broom made of a bundle of twigs; he was also there, and she was teasing him or scolding him" (*SE* 17: 90; *GW* 12: 123–24). Before citing Freud's integral reconstruction of the scene with Grusha, I will add what any reader can easily verify, namely, that there is not a single detail of this memory that escapes analysis: the short broom made of twigs leads to the bundles of firewood where Jan Hus was burned at the stake; this death of the hero by fire leads to enuresis. Here then is how Freud reconstitutes and analyzes the whole of the scene:

> When he saw the girl upon the floor engaged in scrubbing it, and kneeling down, with her buttocks projecting and her back horizontal,

he was faced once again with the attitude which his mother had assumed in the coitus scene. She became his mother to him; he was seized with sexual excitement owing to the activation of this picture; and, like his father (whose action he can only have regarded at the time as urination), he behaved in a masculine way towards her. His urinating on the floor was in reality an attempt at a seduction, and the girl replied to it with a threat of castration, just as though she had understood what he meant. (*SE* 17: 92; *GW* 12: 126)

It becomes clear that Freud finds here, in the scene with Grusha, a possible proof of the reality of the child's witnessing, at a very young age, a coitus "a tergo" between his parents: "the scene with Grusha, the part it played in the analysis, and the effects that followed from it in the patient's life can be most naturally and completely explained if we consider that the primal scene, which may in other cases be a phantasy, was a reality in the present one" (*SE* 17: 96; *GW* 12: 130).

What gives the greatest weight to Freud's hypothesis is surely the constancy and the force of attraction his patient had felt throughout his life at the sight of a kneeling woman, leaning forward on her hands, her buttocks projecting upward. This is how he became enamored of Matrona and it is thus, likewise, that he was seized immediately with an unusually violent desire when he came upon a washerwoman at the edge of a pool, without having even glimpsed her face.

By the very excess of the features it sketches, the example of the Wolf Man, who becomes impassioned instantly with an irrepressible desire at the sight of a crouching woman, presents us with the object in its function as cause of desire as Lacan has isolated it.[7] In this case, indeed, the object has almost the value of fetish.

In order to account for the perfect definition of this object, for the permanence of its power, is it enough to refer, as Freud does, to the impression left by the scene of coitus from behind between his parents, which was in fact witnessed at the age of a year and a half? As we know, Freud constantly asks about the probability of such a reconstruction, he constantly hesitates over the question of whether he is dealing with a phantasmic elaboration based on ordinary observations or, on the contrary, with a real event in the history of the patient. He also wonders "whether a child at the tender age of one and a half could be in a position to take in the perceptions of such a complicated process and to preserve them so accurately in his unconscious" (*SE* 17: 38; *GW* 12: 65). For Freud, there is no doubt that an impression, a kind of indelible trace—the woman's position—had been inscribed and preserved on this occasion. But how and why? That is what is not really spelled out, other than through Freud's recourse, which is more implicit than explicit, to the theory of trauma. A determining condition of the imprint was certainly the fact that this scene was sexual but especially that it was felt to be too "strong," too violent by the little witness. In some sense it was not assimilable by the child's libidinal economy: "his sexual life was positively splintered·up [by the primal scene]" (*SE* 17: 43–44; *GW* 12: 71).

A few lines further, however, one finds this detail concerning two aspects of the scene's traumatic character: "the expression of enjoyment which he saw upon his mother's face did not fit in with [his assumption that the event of which he was a witness was an act of violence] . . . ; he was obliged to recognize that what he was faced by was a process of gratification. What was essentially new for him in his observation of his parents' intercourse was the conviction of the reality of castration" (*SE* 17: 44; *GW* 12: 71).

I would like to propose here a more complete description of this moment, which appears to be the virtual but indelible fixation of an impression, a fixation that, by the same token, presents itself as the irrevocable determination of sexual desire. To do this, moreover, I need only take up again the letter of the lesson taught by the Freudian discovery.

Thus, there is every reason to think that at the age of a year and a half the child was already libidinally tied to his mother and even, in all probability, tied to her in a particularly close way. I consider it in fact to be very probable, if not certain, that when he was quite young he was "seduced" by her and not only by his sister. As a result, he found himself to be invested by her as a little phallus, the letter and object of neurotic maternal desire. His lack of appetite during his first months could well have been a symptom of this.

For the child, this privileged situation, in which he is promoted to the rank of a little god by his mother, also constitutes a closed situation because such a conjuncture effaces, through the intensity of the pleasure achieved, the effect of unsatisfaction from which desire is born. The child-idol thus finds himself caught in a sort of precious reliquary whose shell separates him from any true access to the reality of the letter. In other words, the path of a singular involvement in the order of desire seems to be closed to him.

Having thus quickly sketched the child's libidinal situation, in the framework of the Oedipus complex, we can say that the spectacle of the primal scene is traumatic in the sense that it represents a lover's catastrophe. If this mother for whom he is the cherished object takes pleasure in this way with another, his world falls apart . . . unless he can find a defense against this fatal blow. I believe that in the circumstance his only defense was to cry: "Shit! It's not she." "Shit": that's what he does right away, assumes Freud. "It's not she": that is the stone he sets down so as to ground retrospectively the world he wants to preserve. With this assertion, he negates the identity of his mother and poses the body of a crouching woman as object.

The "It's not she" from which the object emerges in our example supposes that the assertion of an "It's she" has been established. But one may wonder what in fact grounds this formula of recognition, this identification of a person in her singularity. Doubtless it is essentially grounded in the name, "mama" in this case, or in some diminutive, but also and no less necessarily in a series of "identifying marks" such as those listed on identity papers: a black wart on the nose (like the one that appears, later on it is true, on the Wolf Man's mother), the shape of a mouth, a row of teeth, to mention here the elements that play an important role in the history of this patient. These can also be singularities that seem more accidental, like the litany of a complaint: "I cannot go on living like this," the phrase that he heard his mother say to a doctor and that he right away repeated so as to identify with his mother when he happened to soil himself by accident. "She" is this nose, this mouth, these teeth, this complaint, and other details or fragments whose secret enumeration constitutes for every lover, no matter how young, the true evocation of the beloved: a skin texture, the warmth of an arm, a certain spicy perfume, the shape of an eyebrow, the modulation of a voice. To be able to say "It's she" (or "It's he") is to consider as a privileged set this sum of features that are like so many letters or monemes constituting the true and secret name of the loved and desired other.[8] *This name is also the body* conceived of as a set of letters, of erotogenic zones.

Correlatively, the libidinal urgency of the "It's not she," which is formulated here as a disavowal, has to be considered a dislocation, to take up the image with which Freud describes the traumatic effect of the primal scene. It is properly speaking the name of the mother that, as a result of the refusal to accept reality—or the impossibility of accepting it—is "splintered up." The set of traits that we have just described as a name suddenly breaks apart, to be replaced by a single feature, which is truly anonymous: a projecting rump. For the intolerable void left by the dislocation of the name—or the effect of the "no"[9]—an objectal term is substituted that, although it presents no intrinsic articulation, concretizes this opaque unity, which is moreover, as we shall see, well suited to mask the void and at the same time to serve as support for the real. Thus, one can conceive how the projecting buttocks of an anonymous woman become, for the Wolf Man, the chosen term that triggers automatically the cycle of desire. Here the object appears, in its inert finitude, as the concrete element that in correlation with the literal articulation but in the place of the name performs in a central way a stable function in the economy of desire (we will return to this in a later chapter).[10]

The process I am describing here to account for the determination of the object is found, I believe, in a quasi-constant way in the libidinal histories that make for neuroses. What varies is the moment in which the sequence is produced, as well as, of course, the literal articulation itself. Thus, for the masculine homosexual whose object is the penis, the questioning of identity, which arises in diverse circumstances, seems to bear on the father, or more precisely on his name: it's not he. This deconstruction is answered by the choice of the penile object as substitute for the "name of the father" and support of desire.[11] In a still more general fashion, it is quite apparent that, in so-called normal developments, the determination of the sexual object takes part in this process. Thus, a man's elective affinity for a certain type of feminine body always implies, more or less, an "It's not she, my mother," as a mode of assuming the incestuous relation. Likewise, for a woman, man as sexual object results no doubt from an "It's not he, my father."

Upon analysis of this case, the object whose nature we are investigating appears in its essential correlation with the letter. We have already formulated the outline of a theory of these facts,[12] and we will have occasion later to take up again, from a systematic perspective, the question of the relations between the letter and the object.

For the moment, however, let us return to the question of the letter and, specifically, the identification of its mode of presence in the text of the same psychoanalysis. "From the History of an Infantile Neurosis" foregrounds one letter at least, in its most "literal" sense, because of the singularity it assumes for the Wolf Man. Around this letter variations are developed that are played, so to speak, around a single feature. I am referring to the Roman numeral five, the *V* that Freud isolates when his patient evokes once more the movement—which for him is a cause of anxiety—of the butterfly's wings as it lights on a flower:

> the patient remarked that the opening and shutting of the butterfly's wings while it was settled on the flower had given him an uncanny feeling. It had looked, so he said, like a woman opening her legs, and the legs then made the shape of a Roman V, which, as we know, was the hour at which, in his boyhood, and even up to the time of the treatment, he used to fall into a depressed state of mind. (*SE* 17: 90; *GW* 12: 123)

This immediate crossing over from the wings of the butterfly to a woman's legs, then from there to the identification of the fifth hour, illustrates well the literal function of the V.

Thus, this acutely angled trait seems to be, for the Wolf Man, not only the figuration but especially the numeral or the letter of a movement of opening-closing, in the sense in which one speaks of a letter for the combination of a secret lock, or else of the ciphering key to a code. Around this letter, the essential moments of his analysis pivot. The anxiety of the wolf nightmare culminates in the moment when "suddenly the window opened of its own accord," and Freud immediately interprets this moment, basing himself literally on the term *opening*, as, "My eyes suddenly opened" (*SE* 17: 34; *GW* 12: 61). This interpretation refers, then, to the moment of waking when the vision of the primal scene begins, just as the movement of opening marks the moment of waking that puts an end to the nightmare. One could, of course, retain only the figurative sense of this element, but one would thereby risk misrecognizing the essential way in which it functions as a formal marker, or as a "spring" in the unconscious combination, to continue the image of the lock. Moreover, in the text of the dream, as in a poorly concealed secret, this letter seems to insist by itself. First, it insists at the level of graphic literality in the initial W of the German word *Wolf*.[13] Second, it insists at the level of the drawing that the patient produces to represent his dream, where the wide-open, attentive ears of the wolves are drawn as two inverted Vs joined by a line (ʌ_ʌ). Finally, the letter insists again in the fact that only five—that is, V—wolves are represented in the image, whereas in the narration it is a question of six or seven animals. One may consider that "the fear of wolves," in its traditional succinctness, is evoked in the dream as the fear of being eaten by a wolf. This gives the patient the occasion to recall the image of a standing wolf that illustrated the tale of Little Red Riding Hood and whose sight terrified him in his childhood. A recumbent V (<) is, moreover, the hasty representation of an animal's open mouth seen in profile, for instance, that of a wolf or a crocodile. Around the movement of opening and closing, of which V seems to be the figuration as well as the letter, we may already glimpse a multiplicity of determinations, each one concerning a portal of the body, that is, an erotogenic zone.

The opening and closing of the mouth has roots far back in the patient's experience. In his earliest childhood, before the age of three months, he almost died of bronchial pneumonia; according to family legend his shroud had even be readied. At this time he was, if not anorexic, at least difficult to feed, which allows one to suppose that, like many other infants who have been pinned down too early in an impasse of desire as a result of the mother's neurotic love, he played precociously with the possibility of not opening his mouth. And we all know the naive tricks that mothers or nurses use to get a child to open his or her mouth, or even to force a child to close it. Opening the ears, although not closing them, is figured clearly in the dream by the erect ears of the wolves, which are like those of dogs when they are paying attention to something. Thus, one can imagine that the patient was also attentive to something when he was spying in silence, or in feigned sleep, on the gasping respiration that rhythmically accompanied his parents' embrace. Opening, closing the eyes is doubly represented in the dream: on the one hand, by the opening of the window; on the other, by the fixed and immobile stare of the wolves. This opening of the eyes and this contemplation that is both fascinated and fraught with anxiety refer, Freud has no doubt, to the child's looking upon the primal scene of coitus between his parents:

> He had been sleeping in his cot, then, in his parents' bedroom, and woke up, perhaps because of his rising fever, in the afternoon, possibly at five o'clock, the hour which was later marked out by depression. It harmonizes with our assumption that it was a hot summer's day, if we suppose that his parents had retired, half undressed, for an afternoon *siesta*. When he woke up, he witnessed a coitus *a tergo*, three times repeated; he was able to see his mother's genitals as well as his father's member; and he understood the process as well as its significance. Lastly, he interrupted his parents' intercourse in a manner which will be discussed later [he emitted a stool and began to cry]. (*SE* 17: 37–38; *GW* 12: 64)

Opening, closing the eyes, the ears, the mouth seem to be inscribed in this single letter V (or the numeral V), as if the brokenness of the angular trait marked, much more than opening, the impalpable interval that makes for the perceptible moment of the passage from opening to closing. It is in any case one of the effective springs in the unconscious "combination" of the Wolf Man.

Furthermore, the insistence of this letter is also found in the series of Vs and Ws that goes from the wings of the butterfly to the mutilated wings of the wasp (*Wespe*), which he incorrectly calls *Espe*, that is, by his own initials: S.P. (*SE* 17: 94; *GW* 12: 128). One finds it again in the several *Wolfs* or *Wulffs*—a schoolteacher, a doctor, or a dentist—who will mark his existence for various reasons but essentially, it seems, because of the spelling of their names. Moreover, the upside-down W, turned on its head like the phantasmic character erotically manipulated by his nurse (*SE* 17: 20; *GW* 12: 43), constitutes the letter M, whose directly maternal meaning Freud underscores with regard to the forgetting and then the concealment of Matrona, the name of the girl who first bestowed her favors on him—not without, however, transmitting the gonorrhea that marked the beginning of his adult neurosis.

Doubtless one could object that the importance given here to the letter of opening (closing) does not exactly correspond to the way the Freudian procedure progresses, which is certainly true on the face of things. But it is precisely this argument that is going to allow us to specify what the psychoanalyst's procedure consists of in fact. We have already underscored its paradox: floating attention designates precisely the sort of lateral listening that is better able to grasp fringe phenomena, obstacles, or shadows than the exaggeration of a sign in its place or the well-balanced harmony of an elegant argument.

In practical terms, the letter in play will most often remain, at any given moment in the treatment and until the end of the analysis, in the shadow of the margins, a black light made iridescent by the brilliance of the fringe. What can be seen of the analytic procedure in writings and accounts is therefore a kind of disconcerting construction that gives the impression of being both logical and incoherent, serious and fanciful, as arbitrary as it is truthful, presenting ample pretext for right-thinking indignation. To confirm this, one need only look at the first level of the analysis of the Wolf Man's nightmare as Freud spells it out. He proposes a juxtaposition or enumeration of the following fragments: "a real occurrence—dating from a very early period—looking—immobility—sexual problems—castration—his father—something terrible" (*SE* 17: 34; *GW* 12: 60). This is how the analysis proceeds. It does not have the rigor of a homogeneous series or the blind coherence of a well-thought-out discourse, or yet the worthlessness of a bundling of commonplaces. It is a series of elements that appears in the median space where analytic discourse unfolds, between ordinary good sense and the order of the unconscious. In the paragraph that follows this first summary of the givens of the analysis, Freud, with admirable assurance, puts the accent on the nodal point of the dream: "suddenly the window opened of its own accord." And then the analysis pivots and is in turn opened onto a new dimension. The way is now open to the question of the primal scene . . . and its impasses.

Psychoanalysis, therefore, turns out to be in its essence a practice of the letter, insofar as no letter can in fact be abstracted from the libidinal movement of the body that produces it as mark and mask and insofar as the letter cannot as such be demarcated from its corporeal inscription. For the psychoanalyst, the letter is the stigmata of pleasure, that inscription or trait whose proper nature is precisely its capacity to become detached, like an object, from the body on which it is marked. This objective quality of the letter, the capacity to be thus abstracted, is fundamentally joined to another: the quality of being the positive index of an erotogenic difference, the trace "on the home ground" of the interval of pleasure.

The letter thus seems to have a privileged function between the object and the immediacy of erotogenic difference, a distinction that we have established as essential for any truly psychoanalytic approach. On the one hand, the letter can be called an erotogenic zone, a border that limits and fixates in situ the interval where the possibility of pleasure opens up; on the other hand, it is a trait, which, like an object, is detachable from the body that makes it appear. The letter, however, is neither erotogenic zone nor object, even though it seems that we cannot conceive of it except with reference to these two terms. It is distinguished from the erotogenic zone insofar as it is materially apprehensible, whereas the essential part of the erotogenic zone lies in the indiscernible difference of like/unlike from which comes pleasure. It is distinguished from the object insofar as it is not really a piece of the body but more exactly a trait that both constitutes and represents the body's limit. Above all, the letter can be reproduced in its likeness to itself.

The practice of ritual circumcision makes very clear the distinction between these different terms. The severed foreskin perfectly represents the object, at the same time as the scar left by the cut is manifestly inscribed on the penile erotogenic zone. But the letter of the operation, the reality of the cutting, is neither the detached foreskin, except at its edge, nor the trace left on the penis, except as the trace of the erotogenic opening or incision. In fact, one could paradoxically say *the letter is the materiality of the trait in its abstraction*, limit, trace, knife edge as well as linking mark [*trait d'union*]. But the most important thing, the unique character of this trait, is that it can be repeated, similar to itself; it is an index, therefore, of the like and the unlike in which opens up the possibility of the play of desire. We cannot conceal that the question of the "similar to itself" here remains suspended; however, the elements of a response to that question will be evoked in our last chapter.

This is the privilege of the letter: between erotogenic difference and the object, it is that abstract materiality that seems to fixate the syncope of pleasure and that can be repeated. The handling of the letter thus conceived is certainly the most direct access to the economy of pleasure because, as mark of difference, it constitutes the erotogenic body in its coherence.

What would remain to be done is to consider in detail the various forms that the letter can assume since it is quite certain that the 26 characters of the alphabet, although they represent a thoroughly inventoried category of the field, do not suffice—far from it—to cover that field in all its variety. For the moment, we will do no more than emphasize that, for the practitioner, *any materiality abstracted as a formal element from the erotogenic body deserves to be called a letter*, identifiable in its singularity. This letter is, as such, capable of being reproduced, re-evoked, repeated in some way, so as to scan and articulate the chant of desire.

The continuation of our remarks will no doubt serve to shore up this definition by elaborating different forms in which one can identify the letter in its distinction from and intrication with the object: chosen from the variety offered by psychoanalysis, these forms go from the odor of mint to the black star of a pigmented birthmark.

§ 5 The Dream
with the Unicorn

Psychoanalysis, therefore, proves to be a practice of the letter. To illustrate this fact, I would like to relate here a fragment of the analysis of Philippe, a patient in his thirties, which I have already had occasion to report elsewhere.[1] The study of a dream, that "royal road to the unconscious," will take us by the shortest route into the heart of this story. Here is how Philippe relates the "dream with the unicorn":

> The deserted square of a small town, it is odd. I am looking for something. There appears, in bare feet, Liliane whom I don't know and she says to me: "It's been a long time since I saw sand as fine as this." We are in a forest and the trees seem to be strangely colored, in bright primary hues. I think that there are many animals in this forest and, as I am getting ready to say this, a unicorn crosses our path; all three of us walk toward a clearing that we glimpse below us.

Concerning the principal part of its manifest content, the dream takes up an event from the preceding day: Philippe had taken a walk with his niece Anne in a forest where they had played at stalking game and had noticed, near a stream, deer tracks (or as hunters say in French, "pieds" [feet]). As for the pretext of the dream, Philippe tells us it was thirst, which all the same woke him up soon after this dream.[2] In this regard, he adds that his dinner the evening before had consisted of Baltic herring, of which he is particularly fond.

The unicorn dream, as we shall see, accomplishes the desire to drink, and it is the underlying thirst that we will have to investigate in all its implications. Upon first analysis, the dream leads to three childhood memories that are going to make up the several scene changes on the stage where the play of Philippe's thirst will be acted out.

The deserted square on which the dream opens, like a still-empty stage, leads us directly to the heart of the play. The oddness has to do with the feeling that a monument or a fountain is missing from the center of the square. Having been thus evoked, they then emerge from memory, brought together in a monument— the unicorn fountain.[3] This fountain, which has a statue of a unicorn at its summit, is in reality found in the square of a small provincial town where Philippe spent his vacations between the ages of three and five. But it is not just the remarkable figuration of the imaginary animal that is evoked by the square. It also calls up the memory of a familiar gesture, that of joining one's hands along their interior edges so as to form a bowl and then trying to drink from this makeshift cup the water gushing from the fountain. It is a variant of this gesture that we are going to encounter again in the second memory.

It is still vacation time, probably the summer of his fifth year, during a walk in a mountain forest. The fragment of the dream: "It's been a long time since I saw . . . " leads to this second scene. The phrase is literally repeated in a remark made during the walk the day before with Anne: it's been a long time, said Philippe, since he saw heather so thick and brightly colored, perhaps since he was five years old during a summer in Switzerland. This is the same blaze of color found elsewhere in the text of the dream, transposed onto the trunks of the trees. But the event from the walk that marked him was the attempt to imitate one of his older friends who was able to produce the sound of a siren by blowing through the opening formed between the adjoined thumbs of his two cupped palms.

We find another call, more distinctly articulated, in the third memory, which is staged on an Atlantic beach. We are led there by the "fine sand" that complements the day's residue in the dream: "It's been a long time since I saw. . . . " Philippe probably stayed here at the beginning of the same vacation that would lead him eventually to the town with the unicorn (the summer of his third year). One finds here the principal identity of the unknown person in the dream, Liliane. If one breaks the name down and eliminates Anne, who is already identified, there appears Lili, a very close relation by both blood and marriage, who was with him on that beach. The memory chosen to mark this stay is Lili's teasing: because Philippe, during a very hot July, never stopped saying in every situation and in a grave and insistent manner "I'm thirsty," Lili wound up asking him every time she saw him, "So, Philippe, I'm thirsty?" This affectionate kidding became in subsequent years a complicitous greeting, almost a sign of recognition, a formula pronounced with the same grave and falsely desperate tone that expresses above all the expectation of a guaranteed satisfaction: "Philippe, I'm thirsty."

"Upon complete analysis, every dream reveals itself to be the fulfillment of a wish": this is how Freud condenses in one sentence the essence of his discovery concerning the interpretation of dreams. But what is a wish (*Wunsch*) in the Freudian sense, and what is meant by its fulfillment (*Erfüllung*)? We should not consider that such questions have been resolved simply because these terms have become so banal nowadays. Although we are still far from a complete analysis of the unicorn dream, we can already say upon initial approach, which is more intuitive than analytic, that the dream represents Philippe's thirst. We can even go along with Freud and suggest that it accomplishes it, that is, fulfills in its way the wish to drink, to the extent at least that it defers the moment of waking and drinking. One should point out in passing here that, of course, the thirst in question, as well as the wish to drink that precipitates the dream, cannot in any way be reduced to the circumstance that provokes it, which is a contingent thirst, a need to drink following the meal of herring.

Once evoked, the central function of thirst, far from closing down the interpretation, is presented as an open term, as if this thirst avidly demanded that one listen to the literality or the reality of its interrogative appeal. One may then wonder how the appeal "I'm thirsty" is in return settled upon Lili's interpellation and why this wish to drink is placed under the sign of the unicorn.

As one does in the course of an analysis, we will let the memories, images, and words form a chain so as to attempt to follow, in the strict order of its detours, the path that leads to the unconscious.

It did not take Philippe long to say that he did not like the beach, but he said this with such vehemence that it was easy to guess there was some important theme nearby. Indeed, when he calls up that summer by the Atlantic, memories emerge as clearly and vividly as if they were still current, memories that are literally sensitive: the contact of the hot sand over the whole surface of the body, of fresh, wet sand when one played at burying oneself in it, and also of burning sand against the soles of the feet, which is a pleasurable irritation that doubles the biting sensation of the inhospitable metal covering an overheated balcony under the noonday sun. For Philippe, the idea of a beach still calls up the phobia of sand getting into everything—hair, teeth, ears—and to lounge on a beach, for him, means to expose oneself to the annoyance of not being able to get rid of the sand. Days later, he contends, whatever one does, one still finds some sneaky grain of sand that has escaped from the most careful ablutions in fresh water, a grain that all by itself, crunching in silence, grows next to the skin. Thus, there came to the fore one of Philippe's minor symptoms, a real little phobia regarding badly pleated clothes, the stray crumb in bedsheets, hair that gets into the collar after a haircut, a pebble in the shoe. One sees how, with the evocation of the beach, there arises an overly sensitive little nothing, a grain of the unconscious brushing the surface of the skin and putting the nerves on edge, which can on certain occasions drive Philippe to the edge of the most intense irritation, or even to the borders of anxiety.

Another theme in the dream, the foot (Liliane's bare feet), finds on this beach the chosen ground of its traces: tracks (again, "pieds" [feet], in French hunting vocabulary) of the deer seen the day before the dream, which converge on a place for drinking, the stream at the bottom of the valley; marks of bodies on the sand of the beach where the weather is thirsty; and footprints that get filled in on the shifting shore, lose their outline in the very fine sand, and evaporate from the boardwalk where damp feet have walked. The trace that effaces itself, to be sure, but also the trace that remains: thus, on the outskirts of the town with the unicorn, pressed into the rock, two hoofprints of the horse belonging to a legendary prince who, with a desperate jump into a ravine, eluded his pursuers. Philippe loves his feet, thinks them not at all silly, and takes pleasure in their play. There was a time in his childhood when by often walking barefoot he endeavored to develop the epidermis of the soles of his feet, which he dreamed of making as hard as horn so as to be able to walk without injury on the roughest ground, to run on the beach without fear of hidden pitfalls. And no doubt he succeeded in part if one can believe the story of an exploit in which he sees himself under the admiring eyes of his friends rushing down barefoot over the fallen rocks of a glacial hillside. He fulfilled there in a partial fashion the clearly obsessional phantasm of keeping his body protected beneath the covering of an invulnerable hide.

We thus come once again upon that other major term of the dream, the horn decorating the forehead of the fabled animal. The unicorn's meaning as a phallic representation constitutes the common theme of legendary stories: an emblem of fidelity, the unicorn obviously cannot be procured without difficulty, and it is said that he who wants to get hold of one must leave a young virgin as an offering in a lonely forest, since the unicorn after having placed its horn on her lap falls asleep right away. To be sure, no unicorn really exists, anymore than does the horn of a unicorn: its place is taken by the tooth of a narwhal, a superb spur of twisted ivory, which draws its beneficent power precisely from the real-nothing it represents.[4]

On his forehead, in the place corresponding to the horn's implantation, Philippe bears a scar, the trace that remains from a childhood fight or a fall from a tricycle, an indelible mark, like the mark of ritual circumcision on his sex. The trace on the sand, which is a mark of the body, can now be seen on the skin, a mark on the body, a scar into which the phallic emblem and the trait consecrating it send down their roots in a dream.

Concerning scars, we must here relate another scene that Philippe dreamed not long after the encounter with the unicorn and that seems to take up again the theme of hidden pitfalls in the sand of the beach.

> Someone (a boy about twelve years old, it seems) has just slid with one leg into a hole. He is lying on his side and cries very loud as if he were seriously hurt. People (myself included) run to see where the wound is; but there is nothing to see, neither on his knee nor his leg; all one can find, on his foot on the side of his heel, is a visible scratch in the form of a thin red crescent but it is not bleeding. It seems he hurt himself on some object hidden in the hole: thinking it may be a rusty nail, people look for it but find a billhook [*serpe*].

One sees that in this dream the scar (a wound barely open or already closed) has gone from the forehead to the heel, thereby reversing the movement of the horn. One certainly need not be a psychoanalyst to hear in this narration the most direct allusion to the theme of castration. One can likewise guess that the figured agent of the wound, the *serpe*, veils only through the alteration of one letter the identity of the desired castrator, the psychoanalyst, whom the dreamer names or addresses by his first name. One may thus say, with a summary and allusive formula, that the desire motivating the dream is for castration, on the condition that we make clear the psychoanalytic sense of this term.[5]

But let us pause for a moment with Philippe and consider what a scar is: on the skin, a mark, a slight depression, white or pigmented, more or less without sensation, points to what was a scratch, a cut, or even a wound whose two gaping lips had to be dressed, sometimes even sutured; the trace of a violence done to the body, a durable inscription of a painful, sometimes catastrophic irruption. If the horn is a representation, as we said, of a real-nothing, the scar has the privilege of being, on the contrary, the inscription on the body of the interval of a cut, the mark of a gap that could be felt.

Now, Philippe, for whom the integrity of his body is of essential importance, considers a scar above all to be a filling in, a repair, a suture. For this reason, it is indissolubly linked to his mother's passion to protect, close, fulfill, or gratify. The scar, but as well the whole surface of the body, is a reminder for him of the attentive care of which he was the object on the part of a mother impatient to satisfy her passion at the level of bodily needs. Philippe was washed, fed, warmed, cared for in accordance with the excessiveness of the maternal phantasms. And we know what this kind of maternal love hides and manifests by way of unconscious and well-meant destructive tendencies: no cry that is not smothered, so as not to have to listen to it; an overabundance of food, as if he were nothing but a voracious appetite; no thirst that is not immediately drowned. That is why Philippe, filled to the point of bursting, continued to be thirsty!

We would be mistaken, however, if we went along with Philippe when he claims, and tries to make us believe, that he has only cause for complaint in this excess of maternal kindness. One may guess that he was profoundly marked, in a way that is more ineffaceable than any other, by the passionate embrace of this smothering tenderness. Philippe was most certainly his mother's favorite, preferred over his brother, but also no doubt over his father, and on the always veiled horizon of his story one discovers that precocious sexual satisfaction in which Freud recognizes the experience leading to the obsessive's fate.[6] To be chosen, pampered, and (sexually) gratified by his mother is (as we have already seen for the Wolf Man) a blessing and an exile from which it is very difficult to return. Thus, the scar, for Philippe, is above all this mark of the favorite and this closure of the paradisical limbo to which are relegated those who are outside of life, not yet born to desire or already dead, like so many shades of an Oedipus, seduced too early and gratified by their mothers.

With this evocation of the phantasms and desires of his mother, with this position of the favorite, we accede to one of the major themes of Philippe's analysis.

One may at this point better understand the desire that this dream "à la serpe" fulfills. It accomplishes in its own way the wish, which is moreover ambiguous, to see the mark of maternal closure reopened so that finally the pain of exile may be lifted. This is indeed the first idea that occurs to Philippe regarding the strangeness of the cry in the dream: "[the boy] cries very loud"; it is an odd yell, both a cry of terror and an irresistible appeal, which reminds him of the cry, the "kiaï," of the Zen tradition, supposedly capable of resuscitating the dead. Moreover, this cry refers back to a memory not yet mentioned even though it was called up very soon after the relation of the dream: Philippe is eight or nine years old, traveling with his parents and brother. At the end of one leg of the journey, they put up in a fine hotel, and, alone, he explores the grounds around the hotel that seem to extend very far. Then some noisy, excited boys arrive who are older than him (this detail shows up in the dream: "about twelve years old") and who are probably playing cowboys and Indians or cops and robbers. They pretend to attack him; Philippe, panic stricken in the face of this horde, runs away yelling . . . but not just anything: he cries very loud as in the dream, calling for help from Guy, Nicolas, and Gilles, so as to throw off his attackers and make them believe that he too is part of a large gang. But in spite of his fear he is careful not to yell out the most common names—Pierre, Paul, or Jacques—for his cries must seem to be quite specific. He remembers precisely having invoked the name "Serge" (at the time, it would have been Stavisky or Lifar).[7] This memory makes clear the sense of the appeal in the dream and, as I have intimated, confirms the identity of the castrator (or liberator) who is invoked. It also brings us back to those less clearly articulated appeals called up through the memories revived by the dream with the unicorn.

Philippe, captive of his mother's phantasms, is walking by the sea, saying to himself "I'm thirsty." One can imagine the ambiguity of this declaration inasmuch as it seems, on the one hand, to call once again for the mother's gratifying presence and, on the other, to contest at the same time, in its very repetition, the possibility of quenching his thirst by taking it literally. Here the image of Lili is essential; she is set apart from a group of several other women friends, gathered on this beach, exposing their finally unveiled bodies. Lili is small, her form is filled out, and her breasts are large. It is as if Philippe were moved by her, sensing that she will be better able than another to hear his call. He guesses, with as much certainty as confusion, that Lili is more open than the other women who usually surround him, that she is less captive than his mother to archaic phantasms, and that for her a man, even her husband, is a possible lover. It is as if Philippe were meeting a woman for the first time. This "first time" recalls a process of fixation, and one can find in this occurrence what will later constitute for our patient the inclinations, difficulties, and impasses of his choice. Lili, as a woman, shows herself to be a good listener to the seductive "I'm thirsty." Her address in return, "Philippe, I'm thirsty," seems to seal the success of this seduction and to confirm that the complaint or the thirst is finally heard as a call to desire, if not already as desire for Lili. With the warranty it has of being proffered by the mouth of another, the formula "Philippe, I'm thirsty" fixes in place and summarizes a first kind of compromise of Philippe's desire, in that time of hope or moment of opening that was the summer of his third year. "Philippe, I'm thirsty" combines in a few words the following three propositions at least, along with their respective reservations: (1) I am my mother's favorite, loved by her, but as such I am exiled to an imaginary and nostalgic paradise; (2) my call has been heard, but I have found a passive accomplice rather than someone to help me out of it; (3) I can love another woman (or be loved by her), but she is also prohibited. Indeed, one ought to add here that Lili, a close relation of his mother, was married to Jacques, a first cousin of his father, and we will have occasion to return to the role played by this first name in Philippe's history. Let us merely note for the moment that Lili, who was his relative twice over through blood and marriage, on the one hand wards off and represents and on the other hand doubles the dimension of incest that unfolds here anew for Philippe.

Hence, the meaning of this desire to drink begins to be specified: thirst, contrary to what one might think, represents more an appeal to opening than an expectation of some filling (gratification). It lets one see the primordial capture by the mother, Philippe's nostalgia, and his revolt. But one must also say that this first stage of the analytic work has far from exhausted the resources of the dream material. It is also far from having engaged the forces of the libidinal economy whose mechanisms must be unleashed by a deepened analysis. Nothing would be easier than to stop here and perform an interpretive reconstruction based on a few privileged elements. The temptation to understand is strong, especially when the analysis highlights themes that fit rather conveniently into the frame of our knowledge. But if we give in to that temptation, sooner or later comes the realization that, out of haste, we have done nothing more than substitute one construction for another without bringing about any real modifications. By suspending the analysis of the dream, after having exposed its maternal hue, we would have succeeded at best in repainting with the aid of the palette of psychoanalysis the closure that Philippe complains of. There would be many ways to use this palette if one were not under the strict obligation as a psychoanalyst, first, to hear the sensitive points or the strong points in what the patient is saying; second, to respect these points; and finally, to avoid, as it is most appropriate to say in this case, any closed explanation.

We may recall here the manner in which Freud, in his analysis of the Wolf Man's nightmare, sums up his investigation after a first stage of the analysis. He enumerates the sensitive elements in such a way that, were this a strictly graphic representation, they would be set apart with bold-faced letters (the sequence is, moreover, italicized in the text): "*A real occurrence—dating from a very early period—looking—immobility—sexual problems—castration—his father—something terrible*" (*SE* 17: 34; *GW* 12: 60).

The work of analysis consists essentially in identifying or extricating in this way a series of terms whose more or less obvious insistence, which is always perceptible to an attentive ear, reveals that they are from the unconscious. Such work also requires that one maintain a faithful as well as an open ear, the precise recording and the always-renewable bare surface of a complete welcome. On the basis of our analysis of the dream, we can develop a series of terms that are repeated and underscored in the unfolding of the discourse of "free association." In a still more stripped-down manner than Freud's in the given example, we can enumerate here, without adding any phony links, a few key or crossroad words of Philippe's act of saying:

"Lili—soif—plage—trace—peau—pied—corne" [Lili—thirst—beach—trace—skin—foot—horn]. This is how, upon analysis, the unconscious presents itself: a series of terms, which exhibited together create, for whoever has not entered into the detours of analytic discourse, the heteroclite impression of some bric-a-brac devoid of any order. Faced with such a series of heterogeneous elements, the most natural response, from which no one is immune, is to order the set within the frame of a construction whose type varies according to individual taste and ranges from the biological to the symbolic. Experience most often proves, and one cannot insist too much on this point, that by responding without discrimination to the demand to construct (or reconstruct), one loses, as Freud pointed out,[8] the heart of what the patient's discourse is tending to say: there is thus no other way to listen at first than literally. If we therefore consider the utterance of this unconscious chain in its literality, we notice that when its two ends are brought together, the word *licorne* [unicorn] appears.

A monument of Philippe's phantasm and a metonymy of his desire, the *licorne*—through the displacements it figures, through the intervals it assembles and maintains, through its legend, and through the statue that decorates the fountain—says better than any proof the insistence of Philippe's thirst. It marks at the same time a place at which the desire to drink was asserted. At this point in the analysis, where the effigy breaks down into a play of letters, *licorne* indicates clearly the path leading to the true dimension of the unconscious. And yet, if we are not careful, it can also be the ultimate trap along this path. For one may be tempted, as a last resort, to seize upon the pretty composition of the monument and make it perform the filling-in function of any other construction whatsoever. The *licorne*, as mythical object, is particularly well suited for this use. One need only let its elements become arrested in an image. This, however, would go directly counter to the movement of analysis, in which what is important, on the contrary, is to let the intensity of the meaningful echo spread out and exhaust itself in the unfolding of its reverberation, up to the point at which the literal trait can be heard in all its hardness. One must let it resonate like the call of the siren that Philippe endeavored to produce by blowing into the hollow of his joined hands. In its concise trait, *licorne* marks the gesture of drinking and the movement of the two hands pressed together to form a cup, the concave counterpart to the convexity of the breast, a mimed reproduction of a symbol in its original sense: a gesture of offering or supplication, but above all a gesture of mastery through which Philippe fulfills something of his desire.

With the evocation of this gesture, we step truly into the private domain where singularity reigns in its most secret difference. This movement of the hands, however banal it may be when one describes it formally, is thought of by Philippe as irreducibly his own, on the same level as the scar that marks him on his forehead. And here we touch on the limit of the secret, which one inevitably crosses over when relating an analysis, thereby producing a faithful image of the transgression that is psychoanalysis itself. For the description of these singularities outlines something like the proper essence of each individual in his or her most intimate self.

The ideal aim of a psychoanalysis would be to bring out these irreducible traits, the elementary terms where all echoes fall silent. But it is very rare that one even approaches such a draining away of the mirages of meaning through the stripped-down formality of a literal network. With the *licorne*, however, we seem to get quite close to this knot of Philippe's analysis, not so much, as we have just seen, because of the possible meaning of the *licorne* (even though one cannot exclude it) as because of its formal composition.[9]

The next step of the analysis, which must be understood literally in the sense of a movement, allows us to pass irreversibly into that matrix zone of psychic life where meaning is reabsorbed for an instant into a literal formula, the secret replica of the proper name, cipher of the unconscious. A jaculation, here transcribed with the minimum of travesty, seems to have been the secret name of Philippe: "Pôor(d)j'e—li."

It is very rare that one manages in psychoanalysis to receive the confession of these secret formulas, for they are always jealously guarded. Philippe got around to being able to say this name via a path that deserves to be described in detail. It was, then, a question of gestures, like that of putting one's hand together to drink or to whistle, and, through association, of muscular control, as illustrated by two memories. In the one, he sees himself falling backward from a balcony without a ledge and landing on his feet three meters below, after having executed a dangerous back flip, almost as naturally as a practiced diver might have done. In the other, he sees himself likewise falling, but this time from a farmer's wagon in which he was sitting. By means of a similar natural and rapid movement, forward this time in a kind of head-over-heels, he escapes as before, without the least harm, from the threat of the large wooden wheel. "A misstep, a pirouette, and there you are" could be the formula that sums up this sequence of banal clumsiness, followed by an exceptional deftness, and that ends up in the satisfaction of our little guy, intact and standing on his own two feet. We could translate and interpret the formula as "Fortunately I regained control of my fall into the world." In fact—and this is how we got there—the secret formula prefigured, accompanied, or recalled from most distant memory a jubilant movement that consisted in rolling himself into a ball and then unrolling, finding the result pleasing and then starting over. More simply put, it was a kind of somersault or pirouette that like a magic trick could give rise in an instant of pleasure to something new, but also illusory. *Poord' jeli*, in the very scansion of its secret utterance, somersaulting around the central *d'j* and falling back on the jubilation of the *li*, seems to be as much the model as the reproduction of the tumbling movement.

It is interesting to compare Philippe's self-given secret name, "Poordjeli," with the one given to him by his parents: Philippe Georges Elhyani (also transcribed with a minimum of necessary distortion so as to keep secret the patient's real identity but also to preserve all the possibilities of transgression in analysis). One may find in the latter name, although in a more developed form, a rhythm analogous to the scansion of the formula. But whereas the *j(e)* of the jaculation is in the median position, in the name it pivots around the central *or* of *Georges*. It is possible to identify in this formula the constitutive elements of what may also be called a fundamental "Poordjeli" phantasm: *or* and *je* in *Georges*, as we have just pointed out; *li* in both the first and last names; and finally *p(e)* as the syncope that results when *Philippe* and *Georges* are strung together—which is accentuated at the beginning of the formula,— while a *d(e)*, a dental stop (which cannot be elucidated in our transposition) reproduces at the center of *Poordjeli* the syncope of *Philipp(e)' Georges*.[10] One thus finds in Philippe's analysis, as is often the case, this resemblance between a patient's fundamental phantasm and his name.

With the evocation of this secret name, it seems we have reached an end point beyond which we cannot go: as an irreducible model, deprived of meaning, it truly seems to be one of those knots that constitute the unconscious in its singularity.

Nonetheless, the work of the analysis is not at all complete. When it happens that one succeeds in identifying one of these knots as clearly as in this case, another movement of elucidation can take off from there, a kind of analysis in reverse, which shows how meanings come to be formed in the singularity of the unconscious model and how multiple meanings arise out of these literal matrices. Let us spell out once again the terms of the formula "Poordjeli" while enumerating this time, in this analysis in reverse, some of the meaningful forms that branch out from these elements. Thus, on the basis of the formula's initial *po*, one may bring out meanings such as its homonym *peau* [skin], hide, epidermis, envelope, the importance of which we saw in Philippe's libidinal life. One could likewise follow paths opening onto the particularities of this story, through a word such as *pot*, also a homonym, as in *pot à boire* [drinking mug] or *pot de chambre* [chamber pot], or yet again through the affectionate and gently complaining exclamation of "pauvre" [poor] Philippe, in which the mark of the second *or* already appears, veiled in *ovre* by the light caress of a *v*. Moreover, this median *or* is insistent in several major words of Philippe's singular vocabulary: words such as *fort* [big, strong], *mort* [dead, the dead man], and *port* [port] (or *porc* [pig]) have such a common use that one cannot convey how their originality for our patient stands out from everyday banality, how these words cling to his body.[11] In *corne* and *licorne* this originality appears more clearly, as it also does in a variant of the mother's loving nickname, *pauvre trésor* [poor treasure], although with this common exclamation our attempt at imitation can succeed only feebly in rendering the insistence of this *or* in Philippe's discourse. More singular, however, is the movement of reversal, as scanned by the formula, of *cor* into *roc*, *des or* into *roses*. Thus one finds curiously enough another privileged place of his childhood, the "rose garden," which is located in the same city on the other side of the road not far from the fountain with the unicorn. And Philippe talks endlessly about roses,[12] from their smell to the War of the Roses, a mythical place, a mystical theme, the heart between two breasts at the bottom of a gorge.[13]

No less than the *or*, around which it is doubled in *Georges*, the *ge* brought forward again by this *gorge* is a pretext for some spadework along the singular paths of Philippe's unconscious desire. Thus, we recall the *moi-je* [I-me] nickname that was very early pinned on him so as to stigmatize his overly manifest "egotism." This nickname, which is the pejorative counterpart of "Philippe, I'm thirsty," constitutes here a priceless indication, as does the series of words ending in the same syllable: *plage, rage, sage*. But we will emphasize instead the path that is opened by the *j(e)* in the direction of the series of *Jacques*. Jacques is above all the father's older brother, who died before the birth of his namesake, Philippe's older brother. It is also, as we have already mentioned, Lili's husband. But the *je* is especially emphasized in the *je* of Jérémie,[14] the paternal grandfather, who died very prematurely and whose monogrammed initials, "J.E.," on books and suitcases remain the sign of origin or the maker's mark—the figure of the dead father that cannot be erased by the face of the replacement grandfather.

We will not linger any longer in the paths presented by *li* on which the scansion of the secret name finally lands or its repetition in the first and last name, up to the very significant and explicit *lit* [bed] of Lili.

This manner of analysis, which takes off from a literal formula, may seem surprising or part of some gratuitous game if one forgets that it does no more than bring out in reality, and without the least interpretation, the most sensitive terms in the patient's act of speaking. One could even call them "sensitive" in the physical sense of the term.

That one must not settle for the indefinite games of meaning can be best illustrated if we examine the difficulty of a discourse that takes shape in meaning, a difficulty encountered by the analyst at every moment. Thus, when Philippe relates his memories of the beach and the novelty of his gaze on the feminine body, it is the most natural thing in the world to underscore in passing the privileged representation of the "corps de Lili" [Lili's body] in the bright sunshine. Right away, this representation makes sense, and the body, which is other and the other's, imposes itself, leading to the incestuous desire for the mother and to the fantasy of a full-blown fulfillment. The sense of a certain precocious mastery gets added to this, as power of seduction combined with the impotence of a too tender age. But what probably happens when one interprets the representation in this way—along with the well-known order given to the unfolding avenues of meaning—is that once again the major path, the one that would lead to the unconscious phantasm in its non-sense, in other words "Poordjeli," gets closed down for a time.

The question may be posed here concerning the relations maintained between the representation in language "corps de Lili" and the unconscious jaculation "Poordjeli." Going against common sense, I will insist on the fact that *the literal formula gives the representation its singular value* as much as, if not more, the representation "corps de Lili" invests the secret jaculation after the fact by giving it a meaning. As proof, one may go to the linguistic variants that, for Philippe, make sense, from *corps joli* [pretty body] to *trésor chéri* [cherished treasure], passing through *lit de roses* [bed of roses], which contrast in their meaningful multiplicity with the unsurpassable immutability of the literal model "Poordjeli."

There remains to be considered, finally, the manifestly solipsistic character of the secret jaculation. In the movement of jubilation that it connotes, the formula contains an obvious autoerotic dimension and a narcissistic affirmation, which the evocation of the *moi-je* also renders, but more feebly. The articulation of the formula accompanies, evokes, or translates—better yet, it mimes in its utterance—the movement of the somersault that causes to appear, or that leaves as remainder, something more: mere lure of production, a derisive creation, but at the same time a self-affirmation, "well landed" as a result of the operation. In this autoerotic game, the sequence fulfills a narcissistic phantasm of auto-engendering: on the one hand, Philippe, as an expressive mime, plays out this affirmed apparition of himself at the stopping point of the pirouette. On the other hand, through the repetition of the literal articulation, he seems to reach bliss [*jouir*] in the effect of production or engendering that is correlative to the stringing together of the literal terms, as if the articulation of this secret name caused him each time to be born (or reborn) from his own head, on his own initiative, into the world of language and into his own subjectivity. In a word, we could say that Philippe, through the use of the secret formula, attempts each time to annex for himself the scene of his own conception and that he thus rediscovers his primal scene as often as he impugns it.

What Philippe is trying fundamentally to impugn so as to feign mastering it is, in fact, the very dimension of the other's desire, inasmuch as he was no doubt prematurely its object, beneficiary, victim, and remainder. A castoff of paternal desire who finds his only landmark in the maker's mark of the name of the too-soon-departed Jérémie,[15] an object abandoned to the mother's devouring desire, Philippe, as designated in his derisive formula, will from now on have no other concern than to defend against the other's desire, to contest the other as desiring, which is to say to take the other for dead or nonexistent. For he thinks he knows by experience that if he lets himself recognize the other it would mean falling once again (and perhaps this time without any recourse) into the gulf of lack that makes of him someone who desires, where he would be once again toppled, devoured, suffocatingly fulfilled.

This is the impasse of Philippe's desire, which the complete analysis of the dream with the unicorn reveals in its phantasmic ordering.

§ 6 The Unconscious,
or the Order of the Letter

As we have just seen, the practice of analysis supposes a recognition of the nature of the letter such as it appears in the study of the unconscious, as well as a clarification of the rules belonging to its order.

We have defined the letter, let us recall, as the *materiality of the trait in its abstraction from the body, abstraction* being understood both in the ordinary sense and as an operation of detachment from the corporeal surface. The body is thus taken to be the first book in which the trace is inscribed before it is abstracted as trace and hence endowed with its essential attribute of being repeatable as the same, or almost the same, in its elementary materiality.

We had arrived at this formulation at the conclusion of an investigation of what we take to be the major dimension of pleasure. One may perhaps be surprised by this apparently regressive necessity to derive the letter, a "purely formal" element, from the movement of pleasure and to invoke the "erotogenic body" solely, it seems, so as to speak of the letter abstracted from the body in a second moment. It is true that, in the most ordinary and also natural fashion, the letter is presented as precisely that trait whose absolute formalism eliminates all necessity of referring to anything else but other letters, the connections that define it as letter. In other words, it is the set of its possible relations to other letters that characterizes it as such to the exclusion of all other reference. But one must add here that this altogether admirable concern with restoring the very possibility of analysis by isolating, in a presumed formal "purity," the minimal terms of a logic corresponds in fact, as we will show in what follows, only to an extreme form of misrecognition [*méconnaissance*]. It is the misrecognition that derives from a systematic refusal to recognize that the whole of psychic life, and thus of any logical elaboration,[1] is constituted by the reality of repression. If, as we have already asserted, the trait of the letter is "originarily" drawn as a bar that fixates and annuls *jouissance*, it suffices in fact to let oneself be carried along by this essentially "repressing" function of the letter in order, at the other end of the trajectory, to take it as a term that is "pure" of any sexual implication.

Let us be clear: it is not at all a question of disputing the correctness of the formal point of view, that is, the literal nature of the letter, but on the contrary of giving its full value to its defining formal character. In other words, it is a matter of underscoring the contradictory nature of "abstract materiality." This is not an easy matter because, although no one ordinarily has trouble recognizing the abstract value that allows for the indefinite repetition of the letter and leaves it always the same (or almost) as itself, there is a tendency, no doubt as an effect of some repression, to misrecognize the materiality that defines it, the materiality whose necessary reference to the object, and therefore to the body, is made to appear by the letter. Such a reference takes nothing away from the "formal" character of the order of the letter; it merely underscores the constitutive antinomy of the element that grounds its possibility.

The emphasis we are putting on the paradox of the letter's nature is going to allow us to initiate a further step in our investigation of the unconscious. The study of a literal order tends customarily to be limited to the highlighting of the articulations that preside over the organization of a set made up, for example, of the terms *A*, *C*, and *F*. The supplement we bring to this study concerns the process of determination or choice of *A*, *C*, *F* rather than *B*, *D*, or *E* in order to constitute some particular unconscious kernel. The next step in our procedure consists, therefore, in interrogating the fact of "fixation"—which we have already mentioned several times—or the determination of one element rather than some other.

Let us recall in this regard the analysis of Philippe. At the conclusion of the study of the dream with the unicorn, the literal formula "Poordjeli" appeared to be an unsurpassable point or irreducible term, with the result that we were able to say paradoxically that this formula permitted a linguistic representation, for example "joli corps de Lili [Lili's pretty body]," to be affected with some semantic value. The secret jaculation or literal formula is unquestionably presented as one of the constitutive elements of Philippe's unconscious, which in no way excludes the possibility that a resumption of the analysis might uncover other such elements. One can say with certainty only that the set of monemes forming *Poordjeli* makes sense, has some "meaning" or other. At the very most one can say, as the analysis showed, that this formula seems to connote originally a jumping exercise, a somersault, which when it is performed with mastery engenders a movement of jubilation that calls for its repetition or, failing that, its evocation through the repetition of the formula. What the preceding analysis has clearly shown, we hope, is the force or insistence of the jaculation's formal character, its truly "formative" value: we are thus reminded of its rhythm turning around the syncope, which is scanned by the somersault, or yet again of its phonetic modulation around which develop precisely those linguistic formulas that are more or less homophonic with it: *trésor chéri, joli corps de Lili, pauvre Philippe.*

One must observe, however, that the work of analysis has remained up to now almost silent about the way in which the traits thus isolated come to be fixed in that immutability we have remarked. To be sure, by analyzing the relations of the formula (or secret name) with the subject's proper name, we have already considered why it is *Poor, d'j,* and *li,* among other monemes, that have gotten fixed. What we have not investigated, however, and for good reason, is the very process of this fixation around the movement of jubilation. To try to say more about this, we must now abandon the strict paths of the psychoanalysis of the neuroses and take up the complementary work of theoretical reconstruction.

The general question being asked, let us recall, is that of the fixation or determination of an element so that it may become specifically constitutive of some unconscious: *V, W,* or *M* for the unconscious of the Wolf Man, *Poordjeli* for that of Philippe. This question may perhaps appear superfluous at first approach, since it is true that, for the practice of the analysis of neuroses, nothing absolutely requires that one pursue any further the "historical" or genetic study of each of the terms. Moreover, from a "purely formal" perspective such as the one we mentioned a moment ago, nothing requires that we elucidate the process of an element's determination since, by definition, its determination is made by the set to which it belongs. Nevertheless, the necessity of the question concerning the determination or fixation of a particular set of constitutive unconscious elements will become clearer if, stepping outside the frame of the analysis of neuroses, we begin to consider what is revealed by the study of the psychotic, and more specifically schizophrenic, fact. In these cases, indeed, one finds a set literally composed of the same elements as the unconscious of the neurotic, but in which no term serves as ballast or center or, more simply put, in which nothing serves as the organizing term. This state corresponds in fact to the absence of an unconscious.[2] Thus, in the schizophrenic, one finds oneself confronted with shadows of letters, each of which refers either indifferently to the set of other letters or exclusively to one of them that seems to take the place of the sexual complement. But upon analysis, there is nothing one can find that truly deserves the name of letter. The materiality of the letter manipulated by the schizophrenic seems to be in fact doubly abstracted from any corporeal reference, so that it is nothing more, finally, than the shadow of a letter, that is, a materiality that refers to nothing other than the materiality of any and all letters.

Thus, for Miranda, the world of her daily life, which she continues to lead with a fragile appearance of normality, is populated, even overpopulated, with "signs." The shape of a hand, a certain fold of clothing, the color of a piece of paper or of a car, a look, words or expressions: these are all "signs" that have at one moment or another concerned her, or even moved her, like her father's left hand lying on the table while he wrote. But today, all these "signs" traverse her as if she could not really recognize any of them since she feels obligated to recognize them all in the inexhaustible network of their possible and, for her, necessary connections. Paradoxically, one could say that if each of these signs concerns her—by the sole fact, for example, that she feels herself to be traversed by them—it is, nevertheless, in an indifferent way.

At most one may recognize in this network that hems her in, or destroys her, a determined intention to annul herself, as if each sign as well as its network aimed at her "physical and moral" destruction. Her native position seems to her to be that of an extermination camp victim. These signs surrounding her surely had for Miranda the value of letters at one time—and still had at the beginning of the period of our treatment—when the physical presence of those close to her maintained her in a sort of pseudoneurotic state whose symptoms—for example, difficulties with sexual orientation—were misleading during a superficial investigation. The hand, the belt buckle, the familiar expressions of her father referred her back to precisely those feelings that bound her to him very intensely. But today, outside this destructive and deadly network, nothing seems any longer capable of concerning her in a differentiated fashion. In Miranda's history, there also appears that typical production of psychotics who have lost control of the letter: the "influencing machine" as Victor Tausk named it with what has become an established expression in the psychiatric vocabulary. This machine is like a new body—Tausk calls it a "sexual apparatus"[3]—whose hallucinatory construction seems to defend against the breakdown of the real body conceived of as erotogenic machine or else as a card on which the programming of unconscious desire must be printed. One may imagine that in these cases the body, considered as a surface on which must "normally" be printed the letters that render it erotogenic, either can no longer receive any traces, like a surface frozen in its virginity, or else submits to some operation that erases them all. The hallucinatory machine then becomes the place of replacement where the letters are inscribed and ordered, and it functions henceforth as a pleasure machine, which is necessarily persecuting or destructive with regard to the disinvested body whose libidinal death it seems, in some way, to decree.

Although the fate of the psychotic seems to bring out more clearly the function of the fixation or determination of some literal element, which is necessary for the true constitution of an unconscious—that is, an order founded on the primacy of *jouissance*—it nonetheless does not enlighten us regarding the specific mechanism of this fixation. We have already remarked that the terms *mark* and *fixation* were used necessarily to describe the installation and especially the almost ineradicable persistence of erotogeneity in some point of the body.[4] We even specified that the inscription on the body was the result of the sexual value projected by another on the place of satisfaction. Thus, as concerns an oral gratification, we emphasized that the satisfaction of hunger had at least to be regarded, in the eyes of the one who gives nourishment, as *jouissance* in order for this portal that is the mouth to be marked by some trait or another as an erotogenic zone and inscribed in the book of the body as a letter of desire's alphabet. Now, although it is relatively easy to conceive of this essential and necessary "project (or projection) of desire" of the other—if only through the most ordinary axis of speech—it seems more difficult to explain the process that culminates in the formal determination of the letter that will be inscribed, in the form of a graphic, acoustic, visual, tactile, or olfactory trait.

We may take it as given that this inscription is produced owing to an experience of pleasure or unpleasure. But we need to describe the process of this inscription in a more detailed fashion.

The question we are asking is important: it is the question of the nature of the connection established between, on the one hand, the perceptible and immediate experience of a *difference*, pleasure or unpleasure described as a difference of tension in Freud's energetic metaphor, and, on the other hand, the trait, mnemic trace, or inscription—an identifiable term of whatever nature. The connection is important insofar as the letter seems to fixate the indiscernibility of the difference and to allow the pleasure it constitutes to be at the very least re-evoked or even repeated. Let us formulate right away the answer, which we will then have to corroborate: the connection that is established is made in the mode of a scanning of the weak beat of a syncope.

We could, of course, take up here the mythical example of the first satisfaction, the naive representation of which always provokes a chorus of hasty approval. But, other than the fact that it is difficult to rejuvenate the example, the description of this conjuncture promotes confusion between the literal function that fixes the interval and the objectal function that comes to mask the gap. The reciprocal articulation of these two functions of the letter and the object, which we have called their intrication, does not presuppose any confusion—quite the contrary.

To develop more clearly what we want to bring out here, let us resort to simple situations, and, as a starting point, why not take a painful circumstance, a sudden rise in tension? In the confusion of pain, bordering on a swoon, that marks the collision against a stony ledge, all that remains, or that continues to be exacerbated, is the sweet smell of the honeysuckle climbing in nearby bushes. It is then as if, in the shock of this near dislocation brought on by the irruption of pain, at the limit of a loss of consciousness the smell of honeysuckle stood out as the only distinct term, which therefore comes to mark the instant immediately preceding the fainting spell or the secondary pain—the very instant in which all coherence seemed to be annulled at the same time as it maintained itself around this mere odor. Conversely, let us represent the syncope of pleasure in an orgasm. If we imagine, for example, someone who unexpectedly grabs the boy who is trying to climb a slippery rope, we may suppose that the twisted cable of the rope in contact with the hands remains, literally, the only point of support that in the event will be able to prevent his falling—as can happen—in the very moment of pleasure. In still more simple terms, imagine the lover with her head thrown back, at the high point of love-making's pleasure, whose lost gaze fixes in her fathomless eye the doubly reversed image outlined in the daylight from the window, by curtains drawn closed but still held in loose tiebacks. With such examples, we will have isolated in its contingency the very trait that seems to fixate the syncope of pleasure.

In all these cases, at the moment difference is produced in the extreme sensitivity of pleasure or pain, a term appears, is sustained, or stands out, which seems to prevent the total vanishing of the instant: the smell of honeysuckle—or else the smell of blood that precedes it—the contour in one's hand of the twist of a rope, the spearheads of light outlined by the curtains: all constitute the form, that is, the letter itself, of the void of pleasure, the only term of this void to remain marked.

Most often in the course of analysis, it is clearly not possible to reconstitute the moment of fixation like this; that moment is thus marked out as a scanning, in counterpoint to the weak beat, of the empty moment of the syncope. This is why the description we have just given of it, even if it seems to us essential, remains nevertheless perfunctory. Many other necessary conjunctions converge in the operation of fixation, among which one can cite without further commentary both the repetition of a series of analogous pleasures (the involvement of the same bodily zones) that are not as yet identified or isolated as such, and especially, as we have already mentioned, the projection of another's desire onto the body taking pleasure. Basing ourselves on the givens of his analysis, we could try here to reconstruct in Philippe's history, and no doubt with some plausibility, the fixation of the initial acoustic form of the formula by imagining the outburst of the mother's tender cry: "Poum, pauvre bout," "Boom, poor little kid."

One may well ask at this point whether the letter, which is thus fixated and constitutes a singular element of the subject's unconscious, is the appearance of a new and original form or whether it constitutes only a new inscription—a sort of appropriation of an already fixated letter as it is drawn in the unconscious of another. In other words, is the acoustic form "Poo" Philippe's invention or did he simply take over a moneme that is already a privileged letter in the maternal unconscious, as our reconstruction would tend to show? In support of this hypothesis, we may recall the Wolf Man's complaint: "I cannot go on living like this," which is a literal borrowing from the mother's discourse. However, despite the examples that shore up the hypothesis of the borrowed letter, I do not think that the fixation of a letter, the recording of a form, is always the result of a simple transcription. Not only can one consider any new inscription to be already a transformation, a new form, but one must keep open the possibility—not at all excluded by the first hypothesis—of the creation by everyone of new and eminently singular forms, such as, for example, the syncopated form or unstable letter that is the *d'j* in Philippe's formula. This possibility is entertained on the condition, of course, that one does not make of this new design an ex nihilo creation but takes it merely for what it is: the investment as letter (abstract materiality) or literalization of a form that was accidentally privileged in the course of a libidinal history. In my view, it deserves nonetheless to be described as a new letter. As we will see in a moment, moreover, this possibility of forming new terms is a necessary characteristic of the unconscious order.

The study of this moment of fixation in any case indicates more clearly *what must be understood by the letter*, in the sense in which it is taken to be constitutive of the unconscious order. It is indeed a matter of a *formally identifiable term*, one whose intrinsic and paradoxical nature is to be this materiality abstracted from the body and distinct from the object. It is the trait that scans the empty moment of a syncope and connotes in another place, in a paradoxical fashion, the indiscernible interval of a difference. It is the trait that fixes in a foreign register what seems incapable of being inscribed, namely, *jouissance* as annulment, which is accomplished in an evanescent fashion by the moment of pleasure.

We have already had occasion to consider the relation of the letter to the two major terms in the economy of pleasure: erotogenic difference and the object.[5] We pointed out that the privilege of the letter consisted in its being—between indiscernible difference and the object—the abstract materiality that can be repeated almost the same as itself. As such, the letter constituted the term whose possible manipulation represented certainly the most direct access to the economy of pleasure. This was already to underscore how much *psychoanalytic research, grounded in the interrogation of the body of jouissance,* leads necessarily to the study of the letter conceived of as an elementary term in the order of the unconscious, the order grounded on *jouissance.*

The attempt to approach the unconscious as order of the letter will now start out again from a new investigation of the fact of *jouissance* in its relations to the subjective function. It is remarkable to observe that the attention we have given to the fixation of the letter makes more apparent the vital point of the economy of pleasure, namely, the syncope, the moment of swooning or vanishing, or better yet annulment. Let us not overlook that it is quite difficult to speak pertinently of this annulment since, by definition, the zero it evokes is in turn really annulled as zero as soon as one speaks of it as a term.[6] This difficulty—which language, by its nature, must assume—would have little more than a speculative interest if *the zero in question were not in fact the reality of jouissance.* What is more, the difficulty highlights the major characteristic of what is called a subject: it is that alternative function capable of engendering in turn its annulment and the effacement of this annulment itself.[7] In other words, the subjective function appears as the one that seems to tolerate or incite the vanishing of *jouissance.* There is no subject conceivable except in this relation of annulment with *jouissance* and no *jouissance* one can speak of outside this relation of oscillation with the subject. In still other, more suggestive terms, borrowed from Lacan, no one can say "I come" except by referring, by means of a misuse intrinsic to language, to a past or future pleasure, the moment in which what vanishes is precisely any possibility of saying.[8]

Regardless of the approach one takes to it, the fact of pleasure makes manifest what Freud described as the reduction of tension, the decrease toward the zero degree of a supposed homeostasis, that is, a relative annulment whose radical horizon would be the irreversibility of *jouissance* aimed at by the erotic dimension in its well-known relations with death.

Let us make clear here that the term *jouissance*,[9] which we use so often, marks for us a kind of primary level of pleasure, which in turn connotes its derived or secondary effects. At this radically unconscious level and from the topical point of view, *jouissance* designates the zero around which is organized the unconscious term (in the triple dimension of literality, objectality, and subjectivity, which we will thematize later). From a dynamic perspective, *jouissance* designates the immediacy of access to "pure difference," which the unconscious structure prevents and accommodates at the same time.

The subject is thus that function, correlative of the letter,[10] that can be defined by the alternative affirmation and effacement of the annulment that is *jouissance*. It grounds the possibility of the letter in the moment of the effacement of the zero and is maintained by the literality of the trait in the other moment in which it vanishes so as to affirm or carry out the zero. By taking up again the term *interval*, which we used to describe the difference setting off the erotogenic zone, we can say that the order of the unconscious or of the letter develops around the pulsation or fundamental oscillation between the affirmation of the interval and its annulment. This is but another way of describing the evocation of the zero and its effacement.

One cannot forget however that in this play between the oscillation of the subject and the trait of the letter a third function, performed by the object, comes to function as a stable point, like the negative of the zero.

Thus a kind of three-dimensional system is uncovered, finally, as the minimal structure of the unconscious order. We hope to have sufficiently shown that *the three terms of letter, object, subject are constitutive of the unconscious properly speaking*. We will have occasion to come back to each of them.

Before continuing our systematic study, however, let us indulge ourselves in a brief digression. Let us consider, as pathologists, the

effect produced by alterations of this structure of a three-sided kernel. On the basis of such variations of the structure, one could no
doubt account for a great number of pathological histories, but we
will mention only two examples of alteration.

The first, which has considerable theoretical importance, concerns the signifying use that is readily made of the letter, for one
can easily imagine that it is difficult to hold the letter . . . to the
letter. The literal trait, apparently so simple to grasp, in fact owes
its existence to the most radical zero, that is, the inconceivable, the
void in a spatial metaphor—objectively nothing except perhaps
the very evanescence of an alternative and redoubled annulment.
Hence, it is to be expected that common usage will tend to ground
the pivot-letter otherwise and incorrectly by substituting a thing—
res, an *object*, the negative of nothing—for the alternate nothing it
connotes. The alteration of the literal function is thus complete:
instead of the correlative trait of the possibility of annulment, instead of, in a certain way, the index of the subject, this function
becomes the representative sign of an object. When we discuss repression, we will have occasion to come back to this common and
even banal alteration of the function of the letter.

We will borrow our second example of structural alteration from
Philippe's history. One may consider that the recourse to the syncopated letter *d'j* at the center of the literal formula "Poord'jeli"
underscores, in the singularity of Philippe's unconscious organization, the wish to affirm or rediscover a compromised access to the
play of desire or of the letter. This syncopated letter represents explicitly (even pleonastically) the alternating eclipse of the subject,
just as the motion of the somersault mimes its sequence. Hence,
the alternating terms of presence, disappearance, and reappearance
seem to be reconstructed with the whole body. We can interpret
this singularity through Philippe's libidinal history: everything
seems to have happened for him as though, through the effect of
maternal desire, the "primordial" object that is the body—the ballast or stable function of the structure—had been turned aside
from its objectal function, which is indispensable to the system's
balance. Quite early, in fact, Philippe's very body had been invested

by his mother as letter (more precisely, as phallic letter) and, as such, dispossessed of its quality of object, despite the appearance of extreme concern that this mother had for the body's functions. The alteration described here, which consists of a sort of effacement of the objectal term in favor of the literal term, seems to constitute one of the constants in obsessional histories.[11]

The unconscious, or the order of the letter, is nothing other than the development and diversification of this structure, where the literal element appears in correlation with subjective oscillation around the annulment of *jouissance* and, by the same token, in correlation with the negative complement of nothing—in other words, the object. In sum, *three correlative functions make up the elementary structure of the unconscious: the object as stable function, the subject as function of alternating commutation, and finally the letter as thetic function.* We will comment on each of these.

As we have already pointed out, the object is the thing,[12] *res,* anything whatsoever, considered in an economy of desire as that which comes in the place of the inconceivable interval of pleasure, in the place of the lost letter.[13] Its function is to "fill in the void" in some way, to hide the reality of *jouissance,* but at the same time one may say that its elective relation to the zero makes it into a stable function, an obscure reflection of the immutability of the nothing that it veils. Just as in the singularity of the Wolf Man's example the massive objectality of a feminine rump puts in play the most violent desire, like an appeal from a dizzying void, so too any object in an economy of desire seems to derive its power of attraction from the zero it masks, *from that reality of jouissance that it tempers so as to maintain its difference from death.* As we said earlier, the object is that which can be conceived of in a relation of greatest antinomy to the interval or "pure difference."[14] Practically, as we have seen, the stable function of the object is by preference assumed by the body as a whole or in its parts, but also, by rights and in fact, by anything whatsoever that emphasizes its link to the immutability of the nothing, that is, that performs this "stable function." Although the letter can, in a certain way—that is, as materiality and "detachable" particle—sustain the same relations of concealment with the zero as those we have just described, the object is nevertheless distinguished from the letter by its concrete character and by the impossibility of a reproduction in which it remains identical to itself. Yet, the relations between the literal function and the objectal function are such that the more or less marked effacement of the one in favor of the other is always possible, and even more or less habitual: the letter is turned into an object, for example, when it is made into a sign, as we have already mentioned, and likewise the object can be literalized, which we described at the origin of the obsessional history. One finds a sharper distinction in the opposition of the object's stable function to the function of the subject, which we will now consider.

The function of alternating commutation, which we designated as that of the subject, is no doubt the most difficult to talk about, for one must describe it simultaneously in its two moments. Yet this difficulty could be easily overcome if it were not for the fact that one of these moments turns out to be a perfect antinomy of the other. Indeed, one of the moments of the oscillating pulsation uncovers, beyond any object, the zero or the annulment that is *jouissance*, whereas the other calls up the letter that with its trait seems to fixate the possibility of the same *jouissance*. It is thus clear that in a certain way the trait of the letter strictly annuls the "pure difference" or the "interval" of *jouissance*. In a certain way, it suppresses the absolute of the zero. The subjective function seems to uncover the zero, or the annulment that is *jouissance*, as much to affirm the primacy and the impossibility of saying anything about it as to transgress, at the same time, the absolute of this affirmation. To put it in terms other than those we have already evoked, the subjective function is the one that permits whoever speaks and says, improperly, "I am the one who can have pleasure [*jouir*] with my nondead body" to have nevertheless the possibility of coming [*jouir*] or at least of acceding to some pleasure through the defiles of his or her desire. The subjective function excludes any "substratum": it is this alternation itself. As a suggestive illustration, we might even describe its unsettled play in favor of one of its mo-

ments: the repeated affirmation of the letter in the obsessional series or the reiterated affirmation of the void in the hysterical series.
But one can see how this function of pulsation, which may be considered a nodal point in the economy of pleasure, is as we have just
said difficult to conceptualize. For, besides the fact that we are
speaking of a function requiring no "support" in order to perform,
being in itself this point of alternating commutation, this function
tends to escape the common mode of conceptualization inasmuch
as it continuously sustains—this is the essence of its function—
the most perfect antinomy. This antinomy can be described as the
antinomy of the affirmation of a truth and of its transgression, as
the antinomy of the zero and the one or yet again as the antinomy
of speech and *jouissance*. In a more approximate manner, one could
say that the subjective function is contradiction in itself and that
this particularity makes it in general difficult to conceptualize. We
should not overlook here the well-known text in which Freud attempts to describe the unconscious system and declares that it is
characterized, among other things, by the absence of contradiction.[15] We will not pursue separately the study of the relations between the function of alternative commutation (the subjective
function) and the stable function (of the object). We will merely
underscore once again, before returning to it in the next chapter,
that the subjective function seems to be established essentially in
the mode of a repeated transgression of the function of the concealment of the void so as to evoke annulment in the inconceiv-
ability of its nothing. As for the relations of the subjective function
with that of the letter, we will take these up now in a new reflection on the literal function.

Contrary to the function of alternating commutation, the *thetic*
function of the letter seems to lend itself more easily to conceptualization. It is this function we prefer to talk about when we evoke
the structure of the unconscious order, to the point even of using
the designation "order of the letter" in an almost equivalent fashion to characterize the unconscious. The proper nature of the
thetic function is doubtless to lend itself to conceptual manipulation. It is true, moreover, that the letter in its thetic function nat-

urally constitutes the emblem of the system. Yet one must not overlook the obvious point that every letter supposes another, that is, all the others. Up to now, we have said just about everything there is to say about this thetic function of the letter such as it appears in the practice of psychoanalysis. It is through this function, and it alone, that the practitioner is able to do what he or she does, for it constitutes the sole access to the economy of pleasure (the economy of drives). As we mentioned with regard to the difficult problem of fixation, this does not at all exclude that it may turn out to be necessary and desirable to have correlative recourse, in the case of psychotic organizations, to some manipulation of the object.[16]

We will pause to consider here only one essential point: the relations of the thetic function to the two other functions of the system. In relation to the subjective function of oscillating pulsation, one must insist on the fact of the absolutely necessary correlation between the thetic function of the letter, on the one hand, and the very possibility of the exercise of the function of alternating commutation, on the other. This correlation can best be seen when one considers the moment of affirmation of the zero because such an affirmation necessarily implies that the annulment of the zero be posed as such. In answer to this annulment of the zero, the effacement of the affirmation is required to assure its reappearance. The thetic function of the letter poses this alternation of affirmation and effacement of the zero that is the subject.

In fact, the relation of these two functions brings out the absolutely reciprocal character of the correlation, for one cannot conceive of the alternating function without the thetic function, and vice versa. Above all, however, the perfect reciprocity of these two functions illustrates in an exemplary fashion the mode of correlation in fact established between each pair of functions constituting the system: letter-subject, subject-object, letter-object.

It is necessary to remark above all that if one forgets that the stable function is but the opaque reflection of the nothing that the object affirms without vacillation, then one may easily confuse the stable function of the object with the thetic function of the letter.

Although by definition the thetic function likewise affirms, albeit by "determining," we have just seen that what it seems to affirm is the very vacillation of the subject, its function of oscillating pulsation. To be sure, this thetic function cannot be fulfilled except through reference (which is, moreover, reciprocal) to the stable function that, in an approximate language, renders the zero always present. But it is nevertheless true that the letter poses the oscillation of the subject, whereas by contrast the object marks without vacillating the empty and silent place of *jouissance.*

The unconscious element, such as we were able to identify it by spelling out the formula "Poord'jeli" in the analysis of Philippe, requires therefore that one think of it simultaneously in its three functions. *The unconscious element is not only the literal form in its abstraction but is also and at the same time the object in its opacity and the subject in its oscillation.* If one takes as an example the central term of the formula, *d'j,* one has to think of it at once as (1) effect of a somersaulting body—like those little dolls that are weighted in such a way as to maintain a perpetual balance, in whatever position, always stable and unstable, (2) syncope of the subject around the moment of pleasure that is the moment of reversion, and finally (3) trait of the letter *d'j.* This is to say, in sum, that the literal function of the unconscious element is strictly correlative with the two other functions, subjective oscillation and the irreducibility of the nothing object.

As we have already said, it is nevertheless the case that the thetic function, or literal function, by its very nature, proposes itself as insignia of the unconscious system. For this reason, it lends itself, outside of the unconscious order, to the privileged fate that in radicalizing its abstraction conceals or represses its essential correlation with the subjective and objectal functions.

With this system made up of a function of alternating commutation, a stable function, and a thetic function, it seems to us that one can characterize what is essential to the unconscious order and be justified in naming it after the thetic function: order of the letter. Obviously, what remains is to situate the relations of the unconscious described in this way with an order about which we have said little so far: the conscious order. We will do that in the next chapter. All the same, let us recall here how indispensable this stage is if one is to be able to situate correctly the symptomatic formations with which, in fact, the practitioner is confronted. We must recall this because to put forward as we have just done the exemplary simplicity of a three-term system as a minimal model of the unconscious structure may seem disconcerting,[17] since the approach of the unconscious fact—through the prism of intermediary formations and the irreducibility of the "consciousness effect"—is usually characterized by complexity. We will return later to this effect, whose captives we inescapably are. It is certainly true that a compound made up of object, letter, and subject lends itself too easily to simplistic schematization because the banality of the terms characterizing the three functions can serve as a pretext to disguise the radical originality of their use in the description of the unconscious.

This is the place to mention the effect, in this case, of a crucial logical difficulty, namely: the use of the thetic or literal function in the elaboration of a theoretical discourse can be only relatively abstracted from its essential correlations with the objectal and subjective functions. In simpler terms, let us say that by convention (the nature of which would have to be analyzed) the "subjective" implication of a theoretical discourse is disavowed. It thus seems pointless to claim to have an absolute defense against the risk of banalizing reduction in a description of the unconscious. In wanting to "pose" radically the objectality, literality, or subjectivity of the unconscious order so as to better distinguish its concept from the ordinary meaning of the words in question, one would only initiate a "neurotic" (or perverse) objectalization of the letter, thereby negating in the process the intention that underlies it. To produce concepts of the elements that form the unconscious is above all to *recognize the unconscious origin of the process of conceptualization* (which we will develop later as regards repression) and take account of it in the theoretical elaboration itself.

This brief digression on the proper rules one must follow in the approach to the unconscious fact cannot exempt us from shoring up, with the facts of analytic practice or theoretical elaborations, the heuristic and operational value of the systematic model in three (or four) terms.

In the example of the analysis of Philippe it so happens that a verbal jaculation, a three-termed formula, is uncovered as the minimal unconscious sequence. As we already pointed out in passing, what becomes apparent there is that the unconscious element, such as it may be grasped—or posed—in the unit of the letter, cannot be conceived of outside of its articulation, either manifest or latent, with other letters. We are leaving aside for a brief moment the question posed by the existence of an itemized set of letters, in short, an alphabet.

Let us underscore rather how our systematic model throws new light on things because it accounts for the fact of the elements' organization in a series or a chain. If we conceive of the unconscious elements as being constituted by three functions, then we can represent the linking of terms among themselves in a more differentiated fashion and perhaps account for a more specific mode of articulation. Thus, on the model of the chemical formula of a body, one could assign a stronger or weaker valence to each function of a same element. It would then be possible to recognize different valences for each function of a given element. For example, the *d'j* of Philippe's formula would be endowed with a strong subjective valence whereas its literal function has a weak valence. If one next considered the term *li* as having a strong literal valence and little subjective valence, one could then account for the particular articulation of these two terms because, schematically, an element with a weak subjective function would by preference articulate itself with an element with a strong subjective function. We add that, in this case, a similar analysis of the term *poor* would bring out the prevalence of its objectal function.

In this hypothesis—made possible by the tripolar deployment of each element—the organization of elements in an articulated series or chain finds a justification that, in our view, has advantages over the mere description of the fact of concatenation.

However, let us not overlook the fact that the level of analysis of "purely unconscious" facts brought out by our example cannot be transposed without further adjustment if one wants to approach immediate symptomatic manifestations, such as the *lapsus* or the phantasmic set. In this regard, let us say summarily that the effect of repression in the strict sense—and hence of the return of the repressed—must be studied so that the modes of derivation and alteration undergone by the unconscious elements can be specified before being introduced into the body of a coherent discourse. We will study this in more detail at the end of the next chapter.

We now need to consider the important question of the set of letters necessarily implied by the analysis of one unconscious element or of a series of unconscious elements.

Just as a letter cannot, by definition, be conceived of outside of its articulation with other letters, likewise the specific linking that determines a particular unconscious cannot be conceived of outside the set of the "system of letters." But this raises the very question of how this set should be conceived.[18]

We have already specified sufficiently the fact that the determination or the engenderment of a particular unconscious letter or term depends essentially for each individual on the system itself that is in play in the desire of his or her parents or primary entourage. We thus do not need to reiterate the description of this effect of determination, which is centered, let us remember, around what we called the creation of erotogenic zones.

The existence of an itemized set of letters cannot, in our view, be considered apart from its "origin" or, rather, from its nature. Given that psychoanalysis brings out the nature of the letter as materiality abstracted from the body, nothing prevents us from saying that the letter conceived of in this fashion characterizes the very essence of literality. Nothing prevents this, unless it is the extension of the effect of repression (about which we will have much to say later). We can already foresee the impact of this effect by evoking the dominant intention of desexualization of the letter that presides over such a process. This intention can be identified at the level of the systematic model, where more stress is placed on the letter's distinction from, rather than its correlation with, the objectal and subjective functions.

First, let us pose the following: of the alphabet that can be formed by the set of terms entering into the literal system, one can say equally that it is in the process of endless and never-finished constitution and that it is constituted for all eternity. At this point, however, an essential observation is required: between the "never-finished" and the "constituted for all eternity" there appears the function of lack in the set, "in the place," one could say, of the term that poses (or can pose) the set as such. We already know that the thetic function of the letter (like each of the other poles in its own function) is grounded in the transgressive affirmation of the zero's radicality. Now the annulment seems to have its place marked out as being essential to any possible conception of a set of letters. Before coming back to this later at greater length, one can concretely say that "each one" affirms itself at the same time as it poses the set of the other "each ones" from which it is lacking. Let us note in passing, moreover, that the lack in question had already been evoked, in an imagistic fashion, as the "lost letter" in the place of which the erotogenic zone is opened.

We are led here to invoke something like a tale to clarify our way of conceiving of the set of letters. If one undertakes, for example, to construct a genesis for this set, one may consider the play of desire animating the sexual activity of a first couple—in that activity's double aspect as conception and conceptualization— objectal and literal engenderment. For this "family nucleus," a first alphabet is written that is made up of gestures and words of love or hate. From there, it is easy to conceive of this alphabet's endless enrichment from one generation to the next, and one could even identify in it the doublings, fixations, and divisions marking the institution of tribes, as well as their successive schisms, in histories of war and peace.

Against this genetic vision, however, one may also consider that the fact of sex, in the monotony of its determination, forces everyone to submit to it: this amounts to asserting that, once sexual difference is given, everything is already written. It is certainly this latter way of conceiving of the literal system that prevails today. The set of letters is descriptively posed as existing, period. Our work aims, among other things, to make manifest what such a proposition "forgets" or represses, namely: *there is no letter or set of letters that is conceivable outside an explicitly articulated reference to sexual difference.*

The set of letters may then be described as a body (or book) on which are inscribed the traits that limit *jouissance.* It is this body, in its primary alterity and the constitutive lack of the term naming it, that finds itself implicated when any letter is put in play. This body, or better yet this series of engendered bodies, constitutes that *other* field, at once complete and incomplete, to which any possible literality, objectality, and subjectivity necessarily refer.

As we will show in Chapter 8, it is the very problematic relation of the subjective function to the set of the literal system thus conceived that will permit us to characterize the essentially psychoanalytic dimension of the "transference."

§ 7 Repression and Fixation, or the Articulation of *Jouissance* and the Letter

Freud always held that the unconscious was a primary system rather than a secondary process like the conscious and preconscious systems. It is doubtless not essentially in a genetic sense that one is meant to understand this distinction between primary and secondary. The designated primariness of unconscious processes must above all be thought of as an assertion of their primacy in the logical order. The care we have taken to establish a minimal model of the unconscious structure reflects what we believe to be the Freudian sense of the primary term.

Turning again to our three- (or four-)termed structural model, we will now bring out its precarious nature, which must be added here to the aspect of its primariness. Practically, one has in fact to recognize that the system seems always threatened by a sort of reabsorption into the very annulment whose permanent transgression it performs. This is no doubt the fundamental tendency of the primary system toward its own annulment that Freud identified as the "death drive" and that he maintained in the face of a unanimous chorus of dissent. In a more detailed fashion, one may indeed remark that, in our minimal formalization, the set of reciprocal relations we described tends to maintain around the radical zero a play that produces the zero through the object, represents it with the letter, and conceals it in the alternation of the subject. With the articulation of the letter in speech, the horizon of *jouis-*

sance in annulment is, like blessedness in the word of God, constantly promised and withheld, to be granted only after death. Thus, the letter, the thetic function of an oscillating pulsation, is constantly pulled toward a signifying reduction whereby it is made to represent the object. Likewise, the subjective function of oscillating pulsation is constantly pulled toward the reduction into a stable function, whereby it is given a color for the circumstance that complements the one with which the object is being painted at the moment.

After this reminder of the instability of the oscillating system of the unconscious, which is apparently threatened at every moment with reabsorption, we can now better understand why it tends to call up the parallel organization of a system that is its antinomy and that can supply it in some sense with a less precarious organization. This is what we will call the "consciousness effect." This imagistic formula, however, should not lead one to suppose we have a finalistic aim here. In other, more measured terms, let us say that it is in the very order of the unconscious to induce, as we have just shown, the slippage of the letter toward the sign that is indicative of an object and to engender, out of the subject's function of alternating commutation, a unifying and stable agency that will be called the ego. It is, finally, also in the very nature of the unconscious order to maintain the stable function of the object by letting one "forget," so to speak, that the object derives this stability only from the absoluteness of the zero it masks. From these three derived elements, which are *the sign, the ego,* and *the objective "term"* (as opposed to the "stable function"), a parallel or derived system is organized. This is the secondary system of the conscious-preconscious in Freudian terminology, whose laws are obviously antinomic with those of the primary or original system. We will not say any more about the laws regulating the conscious system for they are all too familiar to everyone, and not just to psychologists. To assert that they are antinomic to the laws of the unconscious will suffice for our purposes here.

If we now continue to situate in this cursory way the psychic organization as a whole, conscious-preconscious on one side and unconscious on the other, we see right away that repression, the barrier or "cornerstone" on which rests the whole edifice of psychoanalysis (and the whole theory of the psychic apparatus),[1] has for its primary function to assure a degree of purity to the unconscious order. Oddly enough, with the term *purity*, we encounter the moralistic language commonly used with regard to repression, insofar as it is generally conceived, in a first approximation, as a process meant to purge the conscious system of some unconscious and libidinal reality and to do so in the name of a moralizing norm for which that reality is unacceptable. In simpler terms, which are opposed to a normalizing (or moralizing) conception, repression appears as the operation that maintains the clear-cut separation between the primary order and the alterations that give rise to the secondary order, at the same time that it assures the articulation of the two systems.

So as to describe more precisely the crucial fact of repression, let us look once again at Philippe's analysis. Having been arrested by the enigmatic effigy produced in a dream of the fabulous unicorn animal and having developed the literal links condensed in the word *Licorne*, the psychoanalytic work brought out the profound unconscious coherence of the formula "Poord'jeli." At what point, one may ask, did the analytic work really lift the barrier of repression and open some access to the unconscious order? It was, in fact, at the point at which attention was drawn to the literal structure of the representation of the "Li-corne." At that moment, the path was opened to the elaborated series that followed: Lili—thirst—beach—trace—skin—foot—horn [Lili—*soif*—*plage*—*trace*—*peau*—*pied*—*corne*]. But if we are more precise about situating this lifting of repression, then we must say that it is at the moment already indicated, in which one manages to set aside the highly significant value of a linguistic representation, such as "joli corps de Lili [Lili's pretty body]," so as to make its literal structure appear. At that moment is produced, in the case of this analysis, what can correctly be called the lifting of repression. This step, in effect, gives access to the unconscious order as such, in a literal formula, "Poordjeli," which is deprived of any meaning but which, in its permanence, is loaded with libidinal imperatives.

As regards the nature of that which actually falls under the rule of repression, there are doubtless two competing conceptions.

On one side, there are solid reasons to think that it is the representation "Lili's pretty body" that bears the brunt of repression. As maternal substitute, Lili constitutes an incestuous, and therefore prohibited, object that the conscious organization must repress into the hidden reaches of the unconscious. In this conception, we clearly see the moralism we evoked a moment ago. It tends to impute to some conscious norm the unacceptability of the incestuous representation, which is condemned finally as bad, immoral, or dangerous. Above all, however, as one can see, such a conception simply takes as given or acquired by use the fact of the prohibition, without really questioning it.

From another side, if one remains as close as possible to the text of the analysis, one can say that what falls under the rule of repression is actually the unconscious jaculation "Poordjeli." At first approach, the reasoning here is less apparent. From the conscious point of view, the formula seems quite "innocent." Why, then, this repression? We will answer that question in a rather abrupt and direct manner: *the formula is repressed because it is unconscious.* Let us explain. The unconscious as such cannot, by definition, have a place in any order other than its own: *the more structurally unconscious an element is,* in the sense in which we have defined it, *the less access can it have to an order in which nothing can receive it,* unless it in turn alters itself. Practically, one must say that this alteration consists most often in a slippage of the literal function toward a signifying value: thus, the letter *li,* by its sole thetic function or representation of the alternating commutation of the subject—through which it remains linked, as a letter, to any other trait that performs the same function—takes on signifying value in the conscious order by representing the object *lit* [bed] and, why not, "le lit de Lili [Lili's bed]." One thus sees that repression, when more rigorously conceived, is nothing other than the limit that separates and articulates the primary order of the unconscious and the secondary system of conscious-preconscious. From a static perspective, it can be compared to a barrier, just as from a dynamic point of view it can be represented as a force of repression or, on the contrary, of defense. In this dynamic sense, one must also then specify whether one is speaking from the point of view of the primary or secondary system, thereby determining whether one makes of it a force that repels—or provokes—the conscious system out of the unconscious order or, on the contrary, a protective agency (in the conscious sense) that represses any element heterogeneous to the derivation belonging to its system.

Here we must make a digression on the nature of the prohibition or interdiction. We raised this question in relation to the first conception of repression but left it unresolved. To be sure, the question seems exemplary of the moral implication attached to the nature of repression. We are going to see, however, why the interdiction is not the consequence of some moral position but is, in its nature, that which grounds the very possibility of a moral dimension. Above all, the nature of the interdiction poses a problem of great importance for a science like psychoanalysis, in which practice as well as theory are centered around the knot of the Oedipus complex, hence of the major interdiction of incest, and . . . its transgression.

Strictly speaking, *the interdiction appears as the barrier of a diction*, that is, as the fact of a literal articulation, written or spoken. But there are still two levels offered to interpretation of this definition of the interdiction. The first and most common level takes the diction or the saying to be a signifying maxim, whose injunction is imperative in the mode of the commandments: thou shalt not kill. This level of interpretation of the nature of the saying as interdiction implies that there is posed simultaneously a whole parade of reasons, either divine or natural, that serve to ground the absolute of the interdiction: thou shalt not kill, because God said so, because you must respect life, because you don't want to be killed in turn by another, because the human species would be threatened with extinction . . . and so on. It is sufficiently apparent that the question, in its grounding, cannot be resolved, only indefinitely displaced by this level of interpretation.

The other level of interpretation holds that the diction or saying itself is a barrier, a limit. The interdiction, then, is the literal articulation in its formality, whether graphic or vocal, because, as we have already indicated following Lacan, it excludes *jouissance*. The one who says interdicts *jouissance* for himself with his saying, or, correlatively, the one who takes pleasure [*jouit*] causes every letter—and every possible saying—to vanish into the absolute of the annulment he celebrates. *The interdiction is the literal articulation considered in its function as limit on jouissance.* But just as one ought not, at this level of the analysis, confuse the letter with the sign, likewise one must recall the distinction between *jouissance* and pleasure. The *jouissance* in question here is the immediacy of access to the "pure difference" that the erotic seeks at the extremity of its border with death, and even sometimes in the annulment of this border. Pleasure is the representation of this access, *jouissance* tempered by the assurance of reversibility within the oscillating and cyclical economy of desire properly speaking.

We have already considered this moment of annulment called *jouissance*, first, when it was a question of describing the fact of pleasure and the interval of the erotogenic zone and, second, in the description of the unconscious structure. In this latter regard, the moment appeared both as the "positive" pole of the object's stable function and as one of the faces of the subject's function of alternating commutation. The never-ending difficulty in evoking this zero function is analogous to the difficulty one may encounter in trying to conceptualize the nonconcept of (pure) difference, the difference that is nevertheless constitutive of any possible conceptuality. What has to be grasped here is that, in the unconscious structure, *this moment of annulment or jouissance presents itself as irreducible reality in the opening out of its nothing.* Or, yet again, it presents itself as *absolute cause* of any possible function, whether stable, alternating, or thetic, in the same sense that in a biological order no life other than mortal life is conceivable. We emphasize in passing that *jouissance* cannot, all the same, be purely and simply confused with death, unless one wants to confuse the unconscious order with the biological one. What we are putting forward here may be summed up in these terms: *jouissance is the cause of the unconscious order*.

One thus sees, however, that although it is correct to assert that saying or diction, as literal articulation, interdicts *jouissance*, one must at the same time consider that *jouissance*, as annulment, erases the saying and installs the transgression by means of which a new saying (or the repetition of the same) will be imperatively called up so that *jouissance* remains possible. One may consider this reciprocal relation of *jouissance* and the letter to be an essential cycle.

The fact of transgression appears here as fundamentally correlative of the dimension of the interdiction. In other terms, *jouissance* and the letter can be thought of as engendering each other reciprocally. The interval, "pure difference," or the annulment, in which we identified the *jouissance* of the body, engender the letter as mark of the erotogenic zone—as we have shown at some length.[2] Correlatively, *jouissance* can be found again only in a movement of transgression of the barrier of literal articulation, the barrier that it has nonetheless engendered. For anyone who wonders about a possible psychoanalytic practice, it is essential to consider this movement of transgression, which finds here its structural definition.

After this long digression on interdiction and transgression, let us return to the crucial fact of repression, which in its primary meaning is the cornerstone of the unconscious order, and in its secondary meaning marks the separation of the unconscious from the conscious-preconscious system.

To lift repression, which is the simplest way to summarize the process of the psychoanalytic act, should therefore strictly speaking be understood as the result of two operations that are more or less distinct in practice.

The first consists in lifting the curtain of the secondary conscious-preconscious order, of letting go, so to speak, one's fascination with a signifying network so as to uncover the literal elements that subtend it and constitute the unconscious structure proper. Thus, in the example of the botanical monograph dream, this first operation consists in raising the term *botanical* over and above the signifying themes of justification and professional rivalry. Through a series of articulations that are both formal and significant, this term will lead to the truth of unconscious desire: *pflücken, entreissen*, to pluck, to tear away. Moreover, one can recognize in this first operation the role played by the empirical procedure of free association, which, through the implicit solicitation of a verbal linking detached from its expressive or signifying necessity, favors the raising of the curtain of secondary repression that tends to separate the conscious-preconscious order from the unconscious order. In fact, the greater part of the practice of analysis unfolds at this level, and there is good reason to say, as Freud did, that the level of secondary repression constitutes repression proper.

The other level of repression, primal or original repression, is truly constitutive of the unconscious order, at the same time that it grounds the possibility of repression proper or secondary repression. In the example of the analysis of Philippe, one may recognize the effect of this originary repression, on the one hand, in the fact that the repetitive jaculation "Poordjeli" evokes a clearly identifiable pleasure and, on the other hand, in the determining function that the formula fulfills in relation to a *jouissance* where the erotogenic organization tends to dissolve. In Freud's analysis, the "bliss" he experienced as he and his young sister tore apart the book of images of a journey through Persia far exceeds in intensity anything that a term like *entreissen*, to tear apart, might ever evoke, even though the very exciting action of tearing out these images is no doubt but an already revised version of some "first" or, at the very least, older rapture. The primal repression separating the absolute of a mythical *jouissance* from its possible repetition through the defile of the letter makes manifest the proper structure of the unconscious order since it articulates—guarantees and defends— the antinomy of *jouissance* and the letter.[3]

The precariousness of the unconscious order, on which we commented previously, is clinically manifested in psychic organizations of the psychotic type. In such cases, it seems that repression has not been put into effect. This is because, on the one hand, the mechanisms proper to the unconscious order manifest themselves in a more or less wide-open fashion—which is the result of a failure of repression proper. And it is also because unconscious structures themselves turn out to be faltering, or at the very least precarious, as if the functions that maintain them were being poorly carried out, which is the result of a failure in originary repression. At this level, which is crucial for any possible comprehension of psychosis, it seems above all that the function of alternating commutation has been profoundly altered, as if it had become stuck at the pole of its opening to annulment. Thus, the stable function and the thetic function are also disturbed, to the point that, as we have already mentioned, the one can no longer be distinguished from the other, and letters are manipulated there like objects or, reciprocally, objects like letters. From the same point of view, one may say either that the psychotic is banished from any *jouissance* or, just as correctly, that for him or her everything is *jouissance*— both of which formulas mark the failure of the "primary" division between the letter and *jouissance*, which is to say, the failure of originary repression. The absence or weakness of conscious organization in these subjects can only be understood as a failure of repression proper, which is the obvious consequence of the failure of "originary repression."[4]

A question of major importance remains: how is originary repression carried out? This question is legitimate and necessary because, as we have just seen, this moment seems to be lacking in the case of psychosis. Freud asked this question and at the same time attempted to answer it in a rather brief and difficult passage of his article on repression.[5] There he describes originary repression as the result of the first refusal by the conscious of a representative of the drive. He says nothing, however, about the mechanism or the cause of this refusal, except perhaps in another passage where these are attributed to counter-investment. With this first refusal, a *fixation* is established, and the representative in question becomes a constitutive and invariable element of the unconscious. In this connection, recall that we already tried (even before having developed the unconscious structure) to approach this major problem for any conception of the repression of the fixation. At that point, we illustrated merely the general economy of the process in the form imposed by psychosis on its theoretical reconstruction.[6]

Our investigation of the nature of originary repression leads us, therefore, to a second and important digression as we continue our study of the essential moment of fixation.

Recall our definition of erotogeneity as difference fixed in its irreducible interval. Recall as well the little scene we described to illustrate this moment of the determination of an erotogenic zone: the softness of the mother's finger playing "innocently," as in lovemaking, which comes to inscribe, in the exquisite dimple it caresses, its mark, a letter in desire's alphabet. The interval is fixed, an erotogenic zone is constituted. In its simplicity, this conjuncture is going to allow us to specify the arrangement necessary for a *fixation* to happen and a division to occur. First of all, the caress of the dimple must be felt as a pleasure, and a difference must be sensed between the two edges of the lovely little depression, an interval that will become marked and that we will reduce for the moment to the formula $D_1 - D_2$, thereby inscribing this interval between two sensitive but not yet erotogenic points of the dimple. Next, for this caress to be so intensely felt as both pleasant and different than the contact with a piece of wool or the back of the child's own hand, the epidermis of the caressing finger must be clearly distinguished as belonging to another body, an interval that we will formulate as $D_b - F_m$, dimple on the baby's side, finger on the mother's side. Finally, so that the latter interval may be truly distinguished in this division of alterity, clearly the principal and absolute condition is that the caressing finger be itself constituted as erotogenic (in the economy of the other's body), an interval that we can formulate as $F^E_1 - F^E_2$, thereby marking the sensed difference, which is for her already erotogenic, of the end of the mother's finger.

We may consider that, in this conjuncture, a division has occurred between, on the one hand, the *jouissance* that is indiscernible in its essence and, on the other, a letter, which can be figured here precisely by the tracing of an index finger and through which the path to the syncope of an analogous pleasure remains open. The operation of division or, from the literal point of view, the process of fixation seems to be, in the circumstance described, the effect of an encounter or conjunction among three kinds of interval: the not yet erotogenic and exquisite sensibility of the dimple $(D_1 - D_2)$, the erotogeneity of the other's finger $(F^E_1 - F^E_2)$, and the difference between them $(D_b - F_m)$.[7] Notice, however that once again none of the intervals can really be considered outside of its relations with the two others: thus, one cannot describe the zones of exquisite sensitivity $(D_1 - D_2)$ outside of the encounter of two bodies $(D_b - F_m)$,[8] and this encounter itself, or this alterity, cannot be articulated in a coherent way without distinguishing the erotogenic difference $(F^E_1 - F^E_2)$ as such. From another angle, however, we may consider that, in this conjuncture of three correlative intervals, erotogenic difference deserves to be particularly distinguished inasmuch as it is intrinsically the bearer of a letter in its originality, as we have already shown. As such a bearer, it is as if this difference were capable of engendering others, in other words, of investing new zones of another body as erotogenic.

We have, therefore, a first part of the answer to the question we were asking about the mechanism of this first fixation or first division by means of which one may describe originary repression: an erotogenic zone must project its interval or the index of its letter onto the sensible difference of another body.

But how is it possible, then, for this operation not to take place or to occur in such a precarious fashion that it seems to remain ineffectual, which is what we supposed must have happened at the origin of psychotic histories? The disturbance can only come from a profound alteration of the erotogenic interval of the mother's body, $F^E_1 - F^E_2$, in our example. It would be exceptional to have to consider a global anesthesia in which the interval $D_1 - D_2$ would be disturbed; exceptional also would be the circumstance of a form of prolonged symbiosis in which the division of alterity is seriously affected.

We must now look more attentively at what we have called the "erotogenic interval of the other's body," for it seems to us that its specific dimension is essential to the effective operation of the division of originary repression. We have described at length, and repeated several times, the interval or the difference that surrounds the limit of the erotogenic zone, as well as the scansion, by a distinctive trait, of its appearance as void or annulment. Before coming to the essential question of this letter, we will pursue a little further our thinking about the "erotogenic interval of the other's body." Looking now at the possible alterations of this interval, we find that we can distinguish two principal sorts here as well.

First, the disturbance of the erotogenic interval, in the context of the neurotic order, can result from the effect of secondary repression. There is nothing more banal than the extreme erotogeneity of an intimate zone veiled beneath a hyperesthesia or an anesthesia, which it does not take an analyst to reawaken to its erotogenic function. But it can happen that the repression is more vigorous and that the whole of the cutaneous covering falls under the sway of its effects. One can then imagine, in the context of our example, how little "inscribing" effect will be produced by the hand of a mother afflicted with such a repression.

Second, we can specify the difference of the psychotic disturbance, in which the erotogeneity of the parental body—the one that must mark the other body of the *infans* with libidinal traits[9]— is, not repressed in some way, but insufficiently "fixated," as if the interval that ought to constitute it were fundamentally uncertain, poorly or not at all fixated.

We see, however, that whatever sort of disturbance may afflict the erotogenic interval of the other's body, there is the same necessity for a letter to attest or guarantee that this other's body is indeed erotogenic and, as such, capable of giving the body of the *infans* access to *jouissance*, to the letter, and hence to speech.

To be sure, one could remark here that, for originary repression to be effectively constituted, a sufficient condition is that the other, to whom falls the task of marking the child in this way, be actually endowed with speech. This would be approximately correct since it is true that any literal articulation attests, in the final analysis, to this primordial division between the letter and *jouissance*. But this way of saying things remains too imprecise because the transmission of erotogeneity, which is a body of *jouissance* as much as it is a letter, cannot in fact be carried out except by a mark made on a body with another body, except by a trait inscribed directly by one body on another body. The agent of this inscription is, as one may guess, the phallus: it is the type of the organ of erotogeneity, no doubt, but also the vector or witness of the function of engendering (commonly called reproduction).

The study of repression, by requiring us to investigate the essential moment of fixation, thus leads us to consider finally the privilege of the phallic function. We are therefore forced to situate better the oft-invoked phallus, the distinctive element of sexual difference in which psychoanalysis chooses to recognize the model of all difference and, therefore, of all possible literality. In using the term *phallus* here, we must underscore the extreme singularity of this word that *designates the penile object*, as body part and organ of copulation, and, *at the same time, a letter*, which may be called the alpha and omega of desire's alphabet. This second, literal implication of the word, which dictates a preference for *phallus* over *penis* in our language, makes evident its altogether exceptional nature as original letter or *letter of the letter*. On the one hand, in effect, the phallus is the trait that, when isolated in its erection like a stele or obelisk, universally symbolizes the sacred and central character of this eminent erotogenic zone; on the other hand, without any other mediation, doubling, or representation, *it is in itself a differential term* that makes a body either male or female.

To understand the expression "letter of the letter" or "original letter," we must first recall the nature of abstract materiality—abstracted *from the body*—by which we defined the literal trait, in the form it presents in the unconscious, namely, the thetic function. We must also recall that every letter inscribes itself at the same time as it poses the set of letters with the lack that it leaves marked there. By its double nature of object–body part and of differential trait, that is, by the fact of the impossible and patent confusion it represents between the object and the trait, the phallus guarantees paradoxically the distinction between the stable and the thetic functions. The division between *jouissance* and speech (literal articulation), in which we recognized the essence of originary repression, finds in the phallic trait the letter constituting it in its possibility, as if this trait demonstrated the interval that becomes confused with it, or as if it fixated, in its singular and universal privilege, the essential difference that makes any literality possible. One could no doubt also see, in the physiological evanescence of its trait, a paradoxical "immediate model" of the subjective function in its vacillation.

To say that the phallus is at once the letter and the stylet that traces the letter is not, however, to assert that it suffices to engender sexually in order to guarantee, on the side of the genitor, some real fulfillment of originary repression. Certainly nothing prevents the exercise of the organic function with complete disregard for any *jouissance* worthy of the name. Nevertheless, the phallic implication in everything related to *jouissance*, that is, in everything related to the affirmation of the letter and to its transgression, derives from the privilege of this body part as, we repeat, in itself a differential term (of the fundamental difference between the sexes) without any other mediation, doubling, or representation.

To comment now on the fact of "the inscription by one body on another body" would be to repeat word for word what we said about the creation of erotogenic zones, namely: concretely, an erotogenic zone is circumscribed on the target body, in this impact of the interval, by the vector of an erotogenic part of the other's body.[10] We would add merely, in the interest of greater precision, that this piece of the other's body can be conceived of only as differential term (letter) and, as such—that is, as piece of the body *and* differential term—it refers necessarily to the phallic term.

By contrast, a few complementary, although still summary remarks are required here concerning the fact of the erotogenization of the genital zones themselves, which brings us to distinguish at the outset the boy's destiny from the girl's. On the feminine side, the real absence of the differential term, which is correlative with its effective presence on the body of the other sex, constitutes a primary disposition that favors the reception of the erotogenic inscription, while offering itself, by reason of this precocious division, to the accumulation of effects of secondary repression. On the masculine side, the real presence of the penis on his own body seems to necessitate a supplementary period in which to realize the differential term as negative on the body of the other sex and, so as to do that, overcome the anxiety linked to the possible loss of the penis. In addition, the properly erotogenic inscription can occur, on the masculine side, only after a more or less long detour, which for this reason escapes most often from the accumulation of effects of secondary repression. From this more or less ancient erotogenic determination, genital *jouissance* seems to retain a profoundly different nature in the man and the woman, a difference which, according to legend, Tiresias could testify to from experience and render in arithmetic terms: "One day when Zeus and Hera were quarreling over whether the man or the woman experienced the greatest pleasure in love-making, they decided to consult Tiresias, the only individual to have experienced both. Without hesitating, Tiresias assured them that if the enjoyment of love was constituted out of ten parts, woman possessed nine and the man only one."[11]

The structural point of view, we should note, is commonly sustained through an exclusion of any question relating to a genesis, in whatever form. Perhaps, therefore, one should recognize that the term *structure*, in its common use, is not altogether correct to describe what surfaces of the unconscious in the singularity of the cases with which the analyst is confronted. Doubtless it is possible, all the same, to describe a structure of the unconscious and that is what we have attempted to do in our own fashion. When approaching the problem of originary repression, however, one soon realizes that one stands at the limit of two modes of possible approach. On the one hand, since the unconscious order exists, one may consider that there is no need to ask why and how this originary division happens: the described structure exists and is articulated precisely to account for the division. But, on the other hand, the psychoanalyst cannot consider such a structural approach sufficient inasmuch as what is important for him or her, above all, is the renewal of this structure in every singular adventure. To retain the term *structural* and use it without reservation in referring to the unconscious and the whole of the psychic apparatus, it suffices obviously to declare that a correctly conceived structural approach intrinsically includes the study of this moment of engendering of *an* unconscious, analogous in its structure and different in its determinations. But one must also, then, draw the consequences from there and include in this point of view the study of the moment of renewal and engendering. This is what we have just done by investigating originary repression and the possibility that, in certain singular cases such as psychoses, the renewal of the structure is not accomplished, thereby engendering another structure—madness— or a psychotic structure in its many varieties.

We see how the study of originary repression, and hence of the function of the phallus, gives us access to what is most essential in the (psychic) structure. Only by accepting this implication of the term *structure* can one find an opening for the possibility of elaborating a theory of psychoanalysis, in other words, a true practice.

In the blocking of the letter or originary repression, which installs the order of desire, reality, and pleasure through the detour of the secondary formations, the unconscious order ensures, promotes, or sustains the possible repetition of *jouissance*. Yet, one must recognize that it also ensures the renewal, for each individual, of the elements that constitute him or her as *an* unconscious. The mechanism of this renewal—or engendering—must be distinguished from that of *repetition* of which the letter, as such, is the chosen means. We have seen that the essential moment in the engendering of a new unconscious is the moment of originary repression, and the description we have given of it made apparent the necessary conjunction of three types of interval: the separation of two bodies, the interval between two points in a sensitive zone of one body, and finally the erotogenic difference of the other body. An encounter takes place here whose particular and, in some sense, unique nature has to do with this conjunction of three types of interval, conjunction being understood in the sense in which in astronomy it takes the conjunction of three terms to produce the phenomenon of an eclipse. If we continued in the register of this spatial and optical analogy, we could consider the three types of interval in play as so many more or less circular dehiscences, each one circumscribed by an opaque surface. The conjunction along a same axis of these three openings produces what one might call the contrary of an eclipse to the extent that what is eclipsed, hidden, or conjured away is precisely the hiding place or the customary occultation that sutures more or less every interval. It is not a question here, quite clearly, of a mechanism of repetition—although that is not necessarily excluded within such an encounter—but indeed of a *conjunction* in which the difference unveiled without mediation in the coincidence of the three intervals appears in its emptiness and seems, as such, to leave an ineradicable mark in a less than certain place, namely, in the interval of two sensitive points. This mechanism, which we will call the *conjunction of differences*, can be distinguished, on the one hand, by its singularity (there is no necessary repetition) and, on the other, by a kind of doubling or, better yet, double doubling of the levels (three levels). The stacking and opacity of these levels—to stay with our spatial and scopic metaphor—produce the conjunction of their dehiscences. The interval that gets "fixated" in this point of exquisite pleasure—the dimple in our example—fulfills its function of *opening* an erotogenic zone for the body that is marked in this way, at the same time that it attests to both the division of alterity and the erotogeneity of the other body.

We can recognize here the other aspect of the phallic function of engendering inasmuch as this "creation" of an erotogenic zone is the very model of the opening of a new chain that will develop in its formal singularity *an* unconscious, which, moreover, is constructed like every other unconscious.

We will add here merely that this aspect of doubling or double doubling, which we described as constitutive of the operation of conjunction, forms no doubt the structural model of all phenomena of duplication and doubling that the gamut of the most common psychopathology presents to everyday observation. Correlatively, this aspect must be invoked—and this time conjointly with mechanisms of repetition—in order to situate correctly normal and pathological phenomena of identification, that is, the process of assuming singularity in the order of the letter. In such a study, one would rediscover the varied play of the repetition of literal traits. Nothing, however, can account for the recognizable permanence of their networks in any one singular history except this moment of *conjunction of difference in which the process of fixation finds its most rigorous and most extensive definition.* In any case, the crucial fact of originary repression (and, therefore, of repression proper) cannot be conceived of unless one elucidates—according to Freud's indication and as we have just tried to do—the fact of "fixation" that constitutes it in the singular adventure of each unconscious.

§ 8 Psychoanalyzing: A Note on Transference and Castration

My interlocutors in fashionable circles readily say to me, "My, how fascinating your job must be, to hear people's confessions, understand them, help them. But tell me, how do you do it?"

"Well, it's not like that, I'm not there, I mean, in my armchair, to listen to secrets, or to help, or even less to understand . . . which doesn't make the work any less interesting, on the contrary."

How to explain that the psychoanalyst, if he is listening, is there above all not to understand, not to let himself be taken in by any signifying intention of the proffered discourse? There is even something scandalous in the assertion, made too complacently at times, of the therapist's indifference regarding the concern to cure, to help, to do some good. Perhaps only psychoanalytic regulars are no longer amazed by what is inconceivable in the situation. The invitation to speak extended to the patient resembles less an opening onto some maieutic advent or cathartic relief than it does the "say 'ah'" of the physician whose ear is listening only for the thoracic resonance of the voice. Just as the physician asks his patient to say some meaningless phrase that could reveal a speech problem, the psychoanalyst incites speech so as to intercept the order or the freedom presiding over the unfolding of its nonsense:

| *On démolit* | They're tearing down |
| *le Cherche-Midi* | the Cherche-Midi |

à quatorze heures   at two o'clock
tout sera dit.   all will be said.[1]

What has one gone looking for? It has been said: in literal articulation, the very essence of speech, one is looking for *the way in which the one who speaks wrestles with his or her jouissance.*

Just as in psychic life two nonsymmetrical sets—on the one hand, an unconscious knot, the determinate combination of a few letters, and, on the other, the theoretical set of all other letters (or the letters of others)—endlessly play on the problem of their articulation, likewise in the analyst's office a play is staged between the couch and the armchair. One must not conclude, however, that the performance is monotonous because the simplicity of the basic structure determines nothing in advance about either the reversals and surprises in the plot or the casting of the roles. We will return to this in a moment. The play of zero and its representation, or the relation of the subject to the lack it underscores in the set of which it is nevertheless a "part," calls up that "primal scene" in which Freud taught us to locate the space of the impossible knowledge concerning the "origin" of "each one." The question asked there, "Who am I?" has some chance, finally, of escaping any answer (which, moreover, even when it defends itself against such an outcome, can only fixate the "subject" in the objective status of being a product of copulation).

At the end of the analysis, the patient will not know any more about who he or she is but only to what he or she is subjected,[2] to which "cipher," as we saw in our examples, he or she is the respondent. There is no other artifice, in psychoanalysis, except the one by which we contrive for the patient the necessary suspension of our "understanding," wherein his or her saying can at last unfold. For a brief time, the chatter or "dialogue" that so thrills well-meaning souls is going to stumble upon a lack of prejudgments (of understanding) and veer into a discourse of the open void.

The time has come to gather together in a more systematic fashion the settings, roles, and costumes of the drama that, in our day, is allegedly played out daily and simultaneously on so many couches at the same time.

Some*one*, in another's presence, speaks. He investigates what he is. Feeling himself to be, with very uneven happiness (or unhappiness), a more or less distinct *one*, he wonders, in his very singular fashion, how he is situated in the network of other "each ones," living or dead, and, in effect, what void would appear were he to disappear or, in other terms, what place his "presence" occupies.

From whatever angle one considers this starting position (and I mean to include the most naive as well as the most knowledgeable descriptions), it is clear that *the psychoanalytic situation questions this nature of the one relative to the lack (zero) that figures, in the set of other ones of which it is a part, the empty place it leaves by being a ONE.*

Here we again come across the set of letters that, at the end of Chapter 6, we evoked in the form of alphabet, body, or book, in which are inscribed and inscribe themselves the traits that, by reason of one sex or the other, limit *jouissance.* What stands out better here, however, is that this set is maintained only by a one that is lacking. The missing term causes the zero to appear, at the same time as the one (of each one) affirms itself in its exclusion or singularity as an essential part of the set from which it is separated.

The analytic situation investigates this articulation of the separated one with the lack, or zero, by which the one is marked in the theoretical set of other ones. In a more imagistic fashion, let us say that there is a restaging in the analyst's office of the articulation of each one with the sexual conjunction from which it was born as part of two other bodies.

Transference is the effect that is installed and elaborated by the situation proper to the psychoanalytic cure. In a formula that derives from Lacan's teaching, which many analysts have now adopted, transference is situated as the effect of a nonresponse to the demand constituted by the patient's speech. A few remarks are necessary here to describe in stricter terms the specific nature of this situation. They will lead us to take up again in more detail the question of the subject.

To put it in the simplest terms, what is to be analyzed in psychic life is the relation of the subject with the theoretical set of letters. If this formula is to take on its full meaning, however, we must recall, on the one hand, that the term *letter* is used in the sense of the thetic function in a system that also includes a stable function and an oscillating function. On the other hand, we must recall that the term *subject* is determined in its relations with what we have called the subjective function of alternating commutation, in the form in which it presents itself in each of the unconscious elements. Thus, in a formula like the "Poordjeli" brought out by the analysis of Philippe, each term is constituted by a subjective function, just as, correlatively, each one persists as object and is posed as letter. Now, just as the cipher of an unconscious is constituted by the articulation of letters, or just as the object of desire is produced by the sum of objectal correlates, likewise what is called *the subject* (by which we mean, of course, subject of the unconscious) *designates the equivalence among the reappearances of the function of alternating commutation in each of the elements of the "formula" or the "cipher."* If we now represent the subjective function as the repeated alternation of an opening and a blocking, one notices that *the subject can be said to be exactly the same* in each of the elements of the series, and in this way it is different from the other functions of the system. Contrary to the objectal term whose "specific mass" or form necessarily differs from one term to another of the formula, contrary as well to the thetic element, that is, the different (and differential) letter or trait in its essence (*poor* is different from *li* and from *d'j*), the subject, as pure function of alternating commutation that does nothing but make appear and disappear, is indeed perfectly the same as itself in each of the terms of the formula, and it remains the same in each of the elements of the theoretical set. *The term subject*, in the unconscious sense, *designates this series of similarities in each one of the elements*, at the same time as it indicates that this "sameness" consists of a simple alternation without any other determination.

Without being able to develop the argument here, we may suppose that this pole of the *Same*, because it constitutes a continuous similarity in the theoretical set of letters, grounds the function of permanence, or even of unity, that has always been imputed to the secondary formation to which it gives rise and which is called the "ego" or the conscious subject, depending on how one formalizes the psychic apparatus.

With any individual, Philippe for example, the subject of the unconscious can be determined, in general and as we have just seen, as the "permanence" or serial similarity of the function of alternating commutation of each unconscious element. In particular, the subject is determined by the subjection of this alternation, to the extent that the latter tends to elicit, in phases but with its characteristic constancy, the *same* formula, "Poordjeli," the *same* cipher, "P.J.L." (if this is how we choose to encrypt the formula), or the *same* phantasm, such as "Philippe-I'm-thirsty."

We can now specify that, when we speak of the relation of the subject of the unconscious to the theoretical set of letters or, more simply, to the world and to others, what is in question is the subjection to *one* formula. We have seen that this formula was organized around a specifically defined determination in the process of its "fixation." Recall that we described it as the effect of the conjunction of three kinds of intervals or lacks, as a sort of eclipse in which the hiding places of three dehiscences have been spirited away in favor of a conjunction along a same axis. It is indeed around a sort of *immediate realization of the zero* (which could be elaborated as mythical primary erogenous experience) that the formula is organized. The sameness of the alternating commutation will be subjected to this formula as permanence, so as to make it appear and disappear.[3] Concretely, then, it is through the mediation of a fixed formula (cipher, object, or phantasm, according to the level of "secondary derivation") that the articulation of the subject of the unconscious with *lack*, and with the essential one missing from the set of letters, is accomplished.

On the basis of this model of a "definition" of the subject and of its relations to the "world and to others" (the theoretical set of letters), one can now describe the field that develops when two "each ones" begin to speak with each other. This will no doubt allow us to specify at the same time, but in a simpler manner, the proper field of the psychoanalytic situation.

Let us therefore imagine—for the pleasure of the fantasy and the convenience of the presentation—an encounter between Freud and Philippe. In the dialogue that ensues on the subject of mountain hikes, which is a favorite pastime for both of them, and after having evoked a few of their preferred sites, they get around to putting into play or conversation some themes arising from their own phantasms. Hence, Freud, for example, with methodical enthusiasm launches into a description of the pleasure of collecting plant specimens, while Philippe responds to this with an evocation of the patience required when one is looking out for game. And so the dialogue continues.

If we encode as *P.W.F.* (picking wild flowers) and *L.F.G.* (looking for game) the phantasmic compromises of each of the interlocutors, we can represent the play of the conversation as the development of a fugue with two themes. We can also examine in any given measure or sequence the contrapuntal articulation of *P.W.F.* and *L.F.G.*, up to their harmonious intrication in the final "stretto," which combines (hillside) meadow and clearing around a stream in a throng of brightly colored flowers and thirsty animals. To the subjection of the one, manifested in his formula, the other responds, in harmonic resonance or contrapuntal continuation, with the production and development of the phantasmic theme to whose formula he is subjected. We may consider that, in this conversation, each one attests or affirms to the other the singular manner he has of being lacking, insofar as each manifests the modes of his fixation while speaking of his pleasures; that is, each manifests his singular relations to a realization or fulfillment of the zero. In fact, this relation to the zero, in its primary state (or its primary letter) remains hidden for greater security (thus, *P.J.L.* for Philippe), and it is only a secondary letter, *L.F.G.*,[4] the armature of the phantasmic compromise, that offers itself as representative of the primary fixation.

In a conversation described in this way, each one makes the

other a party to the formula of his subjection by interesting him in his phantasm, his desire. One can also say that, through the pleasure of speaking, each one confirms his own subjection and reinforces the other in his.

If we now imagine, however, that Freud returns to his armchair and Philippe to the couch in the Berggasse consulting room, a whole other arrangement of the field is going to be put in place because the analyst will silence any manifestation of his subjection. Nothing, however, can prevent (and we will return to this) the way in which the position of analyst, by itself, marks a certain relation of allegiance to the theoretical model supporting his function.

In the space opened up by the interlocutor who keeps silent the patient's speech stumbles and topples into the discourse of the open void we evoked a moment ago.

Transference is what develops in the field of this new space.

Transference accounts for what allows the clearing of the dream not to be (implicitly or explicitly) a response to the rectangle of the hillside meadow dotted with flowers.[5] It leads, on the contrary, to the quadrangle of the square, to the unicorn fountain, to the space of the beach on which traces are imprinted and effaced. In the Berggasse consulting room where we imagine this psychoanalytic encounter taking place, the space of transference is opened to the extent to which the yellow of the "lion's teeth" is extinguished so that the blue of the heather can be lit up, chime with the periwinkles and gentians, and modulate into the purple majesty of the tree trunks.

In the unfolding of the transference, the analyst is presented with the varied play of the patient's subjection around a single theme at the same time as he witnesses the unveiling of the formula's "kinship" with those that, totally unconsciously, preside over the conjunction of the parents. For more than one reason, it is possible to say that the opening of the space of transference leads the patient to the "primal scene" in which is replayed—in the phantasmic mode of the origin or in the theoretical mode of the engendering of the subject (of the unconscious)—the installation of and confrontation with the limit that says, and interdicts, *jouissance.*

There remains the problem, posed already in Chapter 1, of the psychoanalyst's subjection to the theoretical model that determines his position and his function. In the light of what we have just elaborated, we see that it is advisable to reduce radically this supplementary subjection. This is to say that the theoretical model can consist only of a formula in which the radical function of the zero appears prevalent and in which the alternating function of the subject, reduced to its "sameness," is manifested. That is what we are trying to argue in the present elaboration.

There is one term that maintains a privileged relation with the space of lack exposed by transference: the phallus. This is what I already formulated in other terms when I put forward the notion that the phallus can be called the "original letter" or the "letter of the letter."[6] I was implicitly highlighting in this way the essential function of the *phallus* as signifier of the lack of the letter, *the proper name of zero* around which the oscillation of the subject alternates. Recall that it is the double nature of object–body part *and* immediate differential trait that grants the phallus its privilege as universal index of the lack of the letter.[7] As we have seen, by virtue of its double nature, it paradoxically assures the distinction between the stable and thetic functions, which it does through the impossible and patent confusion it produces between the trait and the object.

As object–body part, the penis is, already in childhood, Freud writes,[8] the leading erotogenic zone and constitutes the place of a privileged narcissistic investment. The woman really does lack the penis, and the imagined possibility of its loss for the man introduces into psychoanalysis the word *castration.*

Fundamentally implicated in the oedipal myth, the question of the "reality of castration" constantly appeared to Freud as an insistent and irreducible one, although he never succeeded, in either his theory or his practice, in truly mastering its concept. In the last version of its elaboration, he still invokes the "phantasm of castra-

tion" in its "originary" nature, which grounds the "castration complex" that is invariably present in every analysis, without further
specifying the meaning of the term *castration* in itself.[9]

And yet, the term speaks to the imagination, and its success, one
must concede, has fed the witty eloquence of parlor room psychoanalysts never at a loss for words. Who has not been told, after
having had the misfortune to crush a toe or slice a finger—or even
simply having forgotten his gloves or lost his umbrella—that he
must certainly want to be castrated, or else, just the opposite, that
he must fear castration and that's why he can't give up an old pair
of shoes?

In a certain way, it is correct that any effect of cutting, separation, loss, and more generally any breaching of the sense of bodily
or physical integrity, can evoke castration, since it is true that the
term awakens profound echoes in everyone. Moreover, in the first
decades of the psychoanalytic movement the extension of the notion of castration was such that Freud deemed it necessary, in 1923,
to give it a strict definition by specifying that in his view "the term
'castration complex' ought to be confined to those excitations and
consequences which are bound up with the loss of the *penis*."[10]

What then about this "loss of the penis" connoted by the term
castration as used in expressions like "castration complex," "castration fantasy," "castration anxiety"? Obviously, it cannot be confused with the surgeon's or veterinarian's sense of the term. Castration is a specifically psychoanalytic concept and, as such, cannot
be conceived of except as a function of the properly psychoanalytic
order that is the unconscious. No doubt this is how one ought to
understand the surprising expression "unconscious concept" that
Freud is led to use when qualifying the " 'little one' [*das Kleine*]
that can become separated from the body" and that psychoanalytic
observation brings into such obvious relief.

To isolate the term *castration*, the most natural path for us to follow is to investigate the "loss of the penis" or the "concept of a 'little one' that can become separated from the body" with respect to
the conception of the phallus, which we have already amply elaborated. We then see that the essential relation to the absence (loss or

lack) of the object calls up necessarily, and offers to reflection, the reference to the phallus conceived as the pivotal term in any possible articulation with the annulment of *jouissance*.

In a general fashion, one may say, then, that *castration is to be conceptualized in psychoanalysis as the relations maintained by the phallus, or the letter of the relation to lack, with the set of other letters*. In a particular fashion, the analysis of the castration complex designates the uncovering of the articulation of the subject's singular formula with the privilege of the phallic term. This articulation of castration is crucial to truly situating the psychoanalyst's undertaking.

To bring out clearly the relation of the subject's singular formula to the phallic term, let us recall once again the emphasis we placed on the double function of the phallus, both object and letter. We said that the phallus, as immediate differential term, carries out the unique function in the literal series of being the letter of the letter. We have just seen that, in addition and for the same reasons, it is more strictly defined as *letter of the lack of the letter*.

Now, as for castration in the sense of " 'little one' that can become separated from the body" one must look on the objectal side of the unconscious kernel. We then see that the penile object, as body part, also occupies a privileged position in the "objectal" series inasmuch as it is effectively lacking in the woman. We can thus say that it alone[11] in the series of objects presents itself either as present in the form of supplement or as really absent (or lacking). What thus stands out immediately as regards the proper nature of the object is that it is the stable substitute of lack, absence, or defect, the thing (*res*, nothing [*rien*]) of the zero.

For this reason, the phallus, which we have already considered as "letter of the letter," is also definable as "type of the object" or in still other terms as the guarantee of all possible objectality insofar as it is manifestly and essentially the hiding place of the object's absence.

Castration, in the sense of "loss of the penis" as well as " 'little one' that can become separated from the body," can only be understood in truth by virtue of this status of the phallus and its cru-

cial function. But whereas the phallus as letter (or object) underscores the joint or constitutes the hyphen that commonly represents the fact of articulation, from the standpoint of castration the
accent is placed, as we have just seen, on the space, interval, or lack
(separation, loss) that brings out the privileged articulation between the phallic term and the set of other terms.

Castration thus conceived concerns, then, the essential fact of
articulation insofar as all articulation necessarily puts in play the
relation with the space of lack. The articulation A-B, for example,
joining and separation, can only be conceived of in relation to the
interval figured by the hyphen between the two terms, the space
reserved absolutely for the lack of any term. In a more figurative
manner, let us say of castration that it is the missing peg joining
the terms in a series or set or, on the contrary, that it is the hiatus
or division marking the separation between the elements. Just as
the phallus can be called simultaneously "letter of the letter" and
"type of the object," likewise *castration can be defined as the model
of any possible articulation* insofar as it constitutes the immediate
access to both the rift and its overstepping. The relation of the
phallus to the set of letters—which is castration—makes immediately apparent *what an articulation consists of: a relation to the zero,
an arrangement that allows a relation with the lack.*

One understands that, for this reason and even if it remains
poorly thought through or insufficiently conceptualized, castration
enters into every psychoanalytic process because treatment aims to
clarify, to analyze, the singular *articulation* of each "one" with the
space of the zero that he or she reveals in the set of other "ones."

If castration is indeed, as we maintain, this model of articulation
and, in practice, the putting into play of this relation to the lack,
then we also understand the universal burgeoning of the castration
fantasy in which are staged precisely the agitated feelings relating
to the representation of the loss of the penis. From this perspective, one can say that the phantasmic elaboration, on the one hand,
covers over this relation to the absolute of the zero through the
imaginary unfolding of the dramatic staging. But, on the other

hand, it introduces into the scenario the reestablishment of this lack through the representation of a castration, a renewed and symbolic cutting of the privileged erotic zone.

If, finally, we recall what we said about the fact of *jouissance* as immediacy of access to "pure difference," or to the zero, one may understand how approaching a certain clairvoyance with regard to castration—which is nothing other than the thematization of this relation to zero—can characterize the process of a psychoanalysis, the questioning of the subject of the unconscious in the face of *jouissance*.

There was a time when psychoanalysis had a hellfire-and-brimstone air about it and was, fortunately, an accursed [*maudite*] activity. That's because people still knew what it was: an interrogation of *jouissance*.

The order of the letter, or the unconscious, questioned by analysis performs this exile of *jouissance* at the same time that it promotes the moment of return. The place of *jouissance* is the region of the sacred, the interdicted sanctuary, which should be understood literally as the consecrated, inviolable space barred by a line. What is blessed—*benedictus*, well said—is the doubled and magnified affirmation of the said that sets a barrier before *jouissance* as annulment. And is not the accursed—*maledictus*, badly said— precisely this *diabolical* interrogation concerning the very function of saying? For in the movement it promotes toward *jouissance*, this interrogation—psychoanalysis—puts the said very much in a bad way.

Notes

Chapter 1

1. In Jacques Lacan, *Ecrits: A Selection*, trans. Alan Sheridan (New York: W. W. Norton, 1977), pp. 1–7. [Because this partial translation bears the same title as the original collection of Lacan's essays, I will signal any further references to it by citing the full title, *Ecrits: A Selection*; references to essays not included in the selected translations will be to the original edition of the *Ecrits* (Paris: Editions du Seuil, 1966), and all translations will be my own.—Trans.]

2. In the common psychoanalytic vocabulary, *transference* refers to the staging, within the frame of the relation installed by the treatment, of affective reactions that may be presumed to be the repetition of infantile prototypes transported onto the person of the psychoanalyst. We will make a few adjustments and additions to this simplistic conception in Chapter 8.

3. This hybrid formula, which comes from the field of experimental psychology, has its place in a point of view that defines psychoanalysis as a method meant to induce an "infantile regression" in the patient. On this subject, see I. MacAlpine, "The Development of the Transference," in *Psychoanalytic Quarterly* 19, no. 4 (1950): 501. One finds the description of an analogous sequence in the Kleinian school: "The question now arises whether regression is not the outcome of a failure of the libido to master the destructive impulses and the anxiety aroused by frustration" (Paula Heimann and Susan Isaacs, "Regression," in *Developments in Psycho-Analysis*, ed. Joan Rivière [London: Hogarth Press, 1952], p. 187).

4. The common meaning of the term *frustration* retains only the notion of deprivation of some object of satisfaction. The German term *Versagung*, which is translated by *frustration* implies much more than the French [or English] word the idea of a flaw within a highly symbolized relation: it ranges from the promise to the refusal.

5. In French, "(im)pulsions": "pulsion" is the standard French translation of the Freudian term *Trieb*, which in Strachey's translation in the *Standard Edition* is rendered as "instinct." I will generally translate the French term *pulsion* as "drive."—Trans.

6. "Perhaps there exists, in this painting by Velázquez, the representation as it were, of Classical representation and the definition of the space it opens up to us": Michel Foucault, *The Order of Things: An Archaeology of the Human Sciences* (New York: Vintage, 1970), p. 16.

7. "I have always thought that Magritte's paintings resisted description," writes Louis Scutenaire in the catalog of the exhibition seen by the patient. We must be forgiven our attempts to describe these few paintings, which the curious reader will want to consult at least in reproduction.

8. A small town of the Auxerrois region, on the Yonne River. It is located on the old route between Paris and Lyon and has a church from the Renaissance period.

9. This is an allusion to the Lacanian shorthand *A*, which stands for the "grand Autre" or "Other."—Trans.

10. That is, "a scream," from the verb *crever*, to burst or puncture, but also, in another colloquial usage, to die; *crevant* can also therefore mean "killing, exhausting."—Trans.

11. "Many of my neurotic patients who are under psycho-analytic treatment are regularly in the habit of confirming the fact by a laugh when I have succeeded in giving a faithful picture of their unconscious to their conscious perception; and they laugh even when the content of what is unveiled would by no means justify this" (Sigmund Freud, *Jokes and Their Relation to the Unconscious*, in *The Standard Edition of the Complete Psychological Works*, trans. James Strachey [London: Hogarth Press, 1955–74], 8: 170, n. 1; *Gesammelte Werke* [Frankfurt am Main: S. Fischer Verlag, 1952–68], 6: 194; henceforth abbreviated *SE* and *GW*, respectively).

12. The "phallus," to be sure, but this should be understood in the sense of the limit of what is interdicted, as we will spell out in detail in Chapter 7. In banal terms, it is the impossible response to the question, "Where do children come from?"

13. Lacan, unpublished lecture to the French Psychoanalytic Society, Oct. 21, 1962; the paintings referred to are those like *Telescope, The Human Condition, Key to the Fields*, in which a window, either open or closed, is inscribed.

14. "At the beginning, it was clear that I was replacing her father in her imagination," *SE* 7: 118; *GW* 5: 282.

15. Freud, "From the History of an Infantile Neurosis," *SE* 17: 11; *GW* 12: 35.

16. The "primal scene" (*Urszene*) refers to the representation of a sexual act between the subject's parents, whether it results from direct observation or from phantasmic elaborations.

17. In the debate that opposes him to Adler, but especially to Jung, on the general conception of neurosis, Freud is concerned to demonstrate in an irrefutable manner the determining character of childhood impressions, in all their contingent reality: "What is in dispute, therefore, is the significance of the infantile factor." The case of the Wolf Man allows him to demonstrate the incontestable importance of this infantile factor: "It is for that very reason, indeed, that I have chosen it to report upon," *SE* 17: 54; *GW* 12: 83.

18. S. Bernfeld has shown that the example invoked by Freud is an autobiographical fragment; see "An Unknown Autobiographical Fragment by Freud," in *American Imago* 4 (republished in *Yearbook of Psychoanalysis*, 1947.)

19. This theme will be developed principally in Chapters 7 and 8.

20. "Those elements of the material which already form a connected context will be at the doctor's conscious disposal; the rest, as yet unconnected and in chaotic disorder, seems at first to be submerged, but rises readily into recollection as soon as the patient brings up something new to which it can be related and by which it can be continued": Freud, "Recommendations to Physicians Practising Psycho-Analysis," *SE* 12: 112; *GW* 8: 377–78.

21. Freud,"From the History of an Infantile Neurosis," *SE* 17: 193; *GW* 12: 35.

22. I have followed Alan Sheridan, the translator of Lacan's *Ecrits*, in electing not to translate this key term. To explain this choice, Sheridan writes: " 'Enjoyment' conveys the sense, contained in *jouissance*, of enjoyment of rights, of property, etc. Unfortunately, in modern English, the word has lost the sexual connotation it still retains in French. (*Jouir* is slang for 'to come.') 'Pleasure,' on the other hand, is preempted by

'*plaisir*'—and Lacan uses the two terms quite differently. 'Pleasure' obeys the law of homeostasis that Freud evokes in *Beyond the Pleasure Principle*, whereby, through discharge, the psyche seeks the lowest possible level of tension. '*Jouissance*' transgresses this law and, in that respect, it is *beyond* the pleasure principle." See "Translator's Note," in *Ecrits: A Selection*, p. x.—Trans.

23. See Freud, *Beyond the Pleasure Principle, SE* 18: 59; *GW* 13: 64.

Chapter 2

1. Freud, *The Interpretation of Dreams, SE* 4: 277; *GW* 2: 284.

2. These variant combinations of "deux verres à la mer," two glasses on the sea, carry more or less meaning: "the green and the bitter," "the two and the pair," "the father and the mother," "the perverse [or perverted one] and the wandering soul," "the drinking of the mother and the whole sea to drink [i.e., an impossible task]."—Trans.

3. Important fragments of this reading have already been published in Serge Leclaire, "A propos d'un fantasme de Freud: Note sur la transgression," in *L'Inconscient*, no. 1 (1967): 31–55.

4. Freud, *The Origins of Psychoanalysis: Letters to Wilhelm Fliess*, trans. Eric Mosbacher and James Strachey (New York: Basic Books, 1954), letter 22. Because the translation follows the numbering of the letters in the German edition (*Aus den Anfängen der Psychoanalyse* [London: Imago Publishing, 1950]), further references to this text, abbreviated *OP*, will indicate only this number.

5. See Didier Anzieu, *L'Auto-analyse* (Paris: Presses Universitaires de France, 1959), p. 28.

6. On the development of this formula, see Chapters 5 and 6.

7. Johann Wolfgang von Goethe, *Faust*, part 1, scene 4; quoted in *SE* 4: 283; *GW* 2: 289.

8. On the subject of generations in the Freud family, see Ernest Jones, *The Life and Work of Sigmund Freud* (New York: Basic Books, 1953), chap. 1.

9. As quoted in Jones, *The Life and Work of Sigmund Freud*, 1: 19. [This translation of Jakob Freud's Hebrew inscription seems to be erroneous, or insufficiently literal, in several regards. In *Freud's Moses: Judaism Terminable and Interminable* (New Haven: Yale University Press, 1991), Yosef Hayim Yerushalmi translates the same inscription, in a "deliberately literal, and hence abrasively unliterary" way, as follows:

Son who is dear to me, Shelomah. In the seventh in the days of the years of your life the Spirit of the Lord began to move you and spoke within you: Go, read in my Book that I have written and there will burst open for you the wellsprings of understanding, knowledge, and wisdom. Behold, it is the Book of Books, from which sages have excavated and lawmakers learned knowledge and judgement. A vision of the Almighty did you see; you heard and strove to do, and you soared on the wings of the Spirit.

Since then the book has been stored like the fragments of the tablets in an ark with me. For the day on which your years were filled to five and thirty I have put upon it a cover of new skin and have called it: "Spring up, O well, sing ye unto it!" And I have presented it to you as a memorial and as a reminder of love from your father, who loves you with everlasting love. (p. 71)

Yerushalmi points out as well that "those with an intimate acquaintance of Hebrew texts will recognize immediately that this one is written entirely in *melitzah*, a mosaic of fragments and phrases from the Hebrew Bible as well as from rabbinic literature of the liturgy, fitted together to form a new statement of what the author intends to express at the moment." Jones's transcription, by this criterion, betrays little of the "intimate acquaintance" that Yerushalmi mobilizes in his extended analysis of the inscription. In particular, Jones's version introduces the error of "seventh year of your life" instead of "seventh of the days of the years of your life," which would be an allusion to Sigmund's circumcision. This error, however, cannot be seen to affect significantly Leclaire's analysis, since, as he writes, "the unconscious speaks without regard to time." It does, however, leave one to wonder how that analysis would have been enriched if Leclaire had been able to pick up on the allusion to circumcision. For some clear indications in this direction, see Yerushalmi, pp. 70–74, and Jacques Derrida, "Archive Fever: A Freudian Impression," in *Diacritics* 25 (summer 1995): 19–21.—Trans.]

10. See Chapter 1, n. 18, for Bernfeld.

11. This common name for the dandelion combines syllables that have the sense of "piss-in-bed."—Trans.

12. This hypothesis, which I mentioned in *Cahiers pour l'analyse* 1–2 (Jan. 1966): 6, n. 4, has been confirmed in an article by Herbert Lehmann, "Two Dreams and a Childhood Memory of Freud," in *Journal of the American Psychoanalytic Association* 14, no. 2 (Apr. 1966): 389.

13. Can one assume it was *Meissen* china? Cf. the *Maistollmütz* dream (*SE* 4: 296; *GW* 2: 302) and what I will advance later concerning the term *reissen*.

14. Freud, "Instincts and Their Vicissitudes," *SE* 10: 125; *GW* 10: 217.

15. "Leonardo da Vinci and a Memory of His Childhood," *SE* 11: 82; *GW* 8: 150.

16. Lacan, "Seminar at Sainte-Anne" (1954–63), unpublished.

17. This latter term shows up in the insult *Geiler Jude*, "lecherous Jew."

Chapter 3

1. Freud, "On the History of the Psychoanalytic Movement," *SE* 14: 16; *GW* 10: 54.

2. "We have reason to assume that there is a *primal repression,* a first phase of repression, which consists in the psychical (ideational) representative [*Vorstellungs-Repräsentanz*] of the instinct being denied entrance into the conscious." In "Repression," *SE* 10: 148; *GW* 10: 250.

3. Freud, "The Unconscious," *SE* 14: 177; *GW* 10: 275.

4. "Instincts and Their Vicissitudes," *SE* 10: 120; *GW* 10: 213.

5. Ibid.

6. "The Unconscious," *SE* 14: 186; *GW* 10: 285.

7. In his article "Le Concept freudien de représentant" (*Cahiers pour l'analyse* 5 [Nov.–Dec. 1966]: 37–63), Michel Tort makes the pertinent remark that in Freud's important text "The Unconscious" priority is given to consideration of the fate of representations; repression is thus described, as we have just recalled, as an operation that bears in fact on representations. But he also underscores that, in a slightly earlier text, "Instincts and Their Vicissitudes," it is the drive itself, in its biological implication as movement of the drive, that is given priority. He writes: "'Psychic elaboration,' 'psychic manifestations,' 'representatives' are only conceived by Freud as forms of manifestation of a final reality that is always the energy of a drive. . . . These determinations are conceived as predicates of an originary, ineradicable reality even though one can at least consider them also to be primary" (p. 46). The ambiguity of the concept of representative and the constant recourse to the biological hypostasis are major constants in Freud's thought. They correspond, according to Tort, to

> an indisputable divorce between the elaboration of the clinical experience of the neuroses (or psychoses) and the theory or doctrine of the drives. Freud treated the latter as mythology and argued that its nature was necessarily speculative. . . . This distance is nowhere more evident than in *Beyond the Pleasure Principle,* where the repetition compulsion, which is first analyzed at the signifying level where it manifests itself, is, in a second moment, "grounded" in

an entirely speculative and "biological" theory of the nature of the drive. Once again, representation (*Vorstellung*) and affect are simply the stage on which is "represented" (*repräsentiert*) a play that is mythically acted out at the level of an "organic" drive. (pp. 55–56)

8. "From the point of view of psychoanalysis the exclusive interest felt by men for women is also a problem that needs elucidating and is not a self-evident fact," Freud, "Three Essays on the Theory of Sexuality," *SE* 7: 146, n. 1; *GW* 5: 44, n. 1.

9. Freud, "Fetishism," *SE* 21: 152–53; *GW* 14: 312.

10. "Three Essays," *SE* 7: 231–32; *GW* 5: 132–33.

11. "An essential component of this experience of satisfaction is a particular perception (that of nourishment, in our example) the mnemic image of which remains associated thenceforward with the memory trace of the excitation produced by the need. As a result of the link that has been established, the next time this need arises a psychical impulse will at once emerge which will seek to re-cathect the mnemic image of the perception and to re-evoke the perception itself, that is to say, to re-establish the situation of the original satisfaction. An impulse of this kind is what we call a wish; the reappearance of the perception is the fulfilment of the wish; and the shortest path to the fulfilment of the wish is a path leading direct from the excitation produced by the need to a complete cathexis of the perception. Nothing prevents us from assuming that there was a primitive state of the psychical apparatus in which this path was actually traversed, that is, in which wishing ended in hallucinating" (*SE* 4: 565–66; *GW* 2: 571).

12. Freud, "An Outline of Psychoanalysis," *SE* 23: 151; *GW* 17: 73.

13. Freud, "On Narcissism: An Introduction," *SE* 14: 83; *GW* 10: 150.

14. "Instincts and Their Vicissitudes," *SE* 10: 125; *GW* 10: 217.

15. Jean Laplanche and Jean-Baptiste Pontalis, *The Language of Psychoanalysis*, trans. Donald Nicholson-Smith (London: Hogarth Press, 1973), p. 325.

16. "On Narcissism," *SE* 14: 84; *GW* 10: 150.

17. Lacan, unpublished seminar, May 1965. On the inadequacy of language to sexual reality, however, see J. Nassif, "Comptes rendus," in *Lettres de l'Ecole freudienne* 2 (Apr.–May 1967): 22–23.

18. The expression I am using here for its suggestiveness, which evokes Hegelian "absolute difference," is to be compared rather to the concept of difference (differance) advanced by Jacques Derrida: "It is not a question of a constituted difference here, but rather, before all determination

of content, of the *pure* movement which produces difference. *The (pure) trace is différance.* Although it *does not exist*, although it is never a *being-present* outside of all plenitude, its possibility is by rights anterior to all that one calls sign . . . concept or operation, motor or sensory. . . . It permits the articulation of speech and writing—in the colloquial sense—as it founds the metaphysical opposition between the sensible and the intelligible, then between signifier and signified, expression and content, etc." (*Of Grammatology*, trans. Gayatri Chakravorty Spivak [Baltimore: Johns Hopkins University Press, 1974], 62–63). In fact, despite the obvious difference that separates both my point of departure and my intention from those of Derrida, I remark the proximity of our undertakings (and this will become clearer in what follows), which is signaled by the necessary recourse to this expression. But for the moment, I am not able to summarize this encounter.

19. See Chapter 7.

20. *Objectality* and *objectal* are used throughout to designate the specific quality of object-ness in the psychoanalytic sense being elaborated here.—Trans.

21. The phrase "lettre perdue" is the standard French translation of the title of Poe's famous tale, "The Purloined Letter," to which Lacan devoted a well-known seminar.—Trans.

22. On the question of this object, one may consult D. W. Winnicott, "Transitional Objects and Transitional Phenomena," *International Journal of Psychoanalysis* 34, no. 2 (June 1953): 29–97.

23. "Instincts and Their Vicissitudes," *SE* 10: 122–23; *GW* 10: 215.

24. This character of the object—the fact that, among other things, it cannot be reduced or specularized—which has been brought out by Lacan (in his seminar for the Ecole Pratique des Hautes Etudes at the Ecole Normale Supérieure, unpublished), refers first to the effect of the cut considered from the topological point of view (Jan. 5, 1966); second, to the designation of the unconscious subject as "re-split" [*refendu*]; finally to the division (*sexus, sectus*) of sex (Nov. 16, 1966).

25. These lines allude to the etymological connection between "réel" (real) and "rien" (nothing). Both derive from the Latin *res*.—Trans.

Chapter 4

1. See Chapter 3.

2. See Lacan, "Ouverture de ce recueil," in *Ecrits*, p. 10, and "On a

Question Preliminary to Any Possible Treatment of Psychosis," in *Ecrits: A Selection*, pp. 197–98.

3. Lacan, "Position de l'inconscient," in *Ecrits*, pp. 847–48.

4. One could add here that such a description of a model of this major articulation, the sexual conjunction, opens a possible path toward an investigation of the nature of logical articulations.

5. Lacan, unpublished seminar, May 13, 1964.

6. See Chapter 6.

7. Lacan, "Kant avec Sade," in *Ecrits*, p. 775.

8. The term *moneme* is used by André Martinet to designate the minimal linguistic unit; see his *Elements of General Linguistics*, trans. Elisabeth Palmer (Chicago: University of Chicago Press, 1966), p. 25.

9. The sense here plays on the homonyms in French, "nom" (name) and "non" (no).—Trans.

10. See Chapter 6.

11. On the use of the phrase *name of the father* by Lacan, see, among other texts, his "The Subversion of the Subject and the Dialectic of Desire in the Freudian Unconscious," in *Ecrits: A Selection*, p. 310 and note, and "La Science et la vérité," in *Ecrits*, p. 874 and note.

12. See Chapters 3 and 4.

13. Here one may remark, in passing by way of this Latin detour, that the insistence of the V would put *vulpus* in the place of *lupus*. This could help with the interpretation of the drawing of the dream, in which the wolves look in fact like foxes.

Chapter 5

1. See Jean Laplanche and Serge Leclaire, "L'Inconscient, une étude psychanalytique," in *L'Inconscient* (Paris: Desclée de Brouwer, 1966), pp. 95–130 and 170–77.

2. The dream, which is the "guardian of sleep" in Freud's phrase, does not altogether fulfill this function to the extent that the sleeper awakes anyway.

3. Philippe knew the series of six tapestries known as the *The Lady and the Unicorn* [*La Dame à la licorne*], which one can see at the Cluny Museum in Paris. But I cannot say whether he also knew the next series (likewise of six tapestries) called *The Hunt for the Unicorn*, which is on exhibit at the New York Metropolitan Museum (Cloisters). The second tapestry in this series, "The Unicorn at the Fountain," represents a kneel-

ing unicorn as it dips the tip of its horn into water flowing in a rivulet from a fountain.

4. In French, "real-nothing" is "le rien réel"; there would be at least three ways to translate this phrase: "the nothing real," "the real nothing," or "the real little almost-nothing (which is thus something)." I will adopt throughout the hyphenated *real-nothing* so as to signal when this phrase is being used. See also Chapter 3, n. 25.—Trans.

5. On this subject, see Chapter 8.

6. *OP*, 30, 31, 33.

7. Alexandre (Serge) Stavisky, 1886–1934, whose name has remained associated with the "affair" of a financial swindle that brought down a government of the French Third Republic in the early 1930's; Serge Lifar, 1905–86, was a highly acclaimed dancer with Sergei Diaghilev's Ballets Russes and director and chief choreographer of the Paris Opera Ballet beginning in 1929. These referents of the proper name *Serge*, in other words, situate the event from Philippe's childhood in the early to mid-1930's at the earliest.—Trans.

8. See Chapter 1.

9. One could observe here that "li-corne," referring to the developed sequence of "Lili-corne," reintroduces at the level of each of these terms the "echoes of meaning." This is correct, and we will have occasion later to return to what seems to be an objection here.

10. The syncope refers to the mute *e* ending of *Philippe* when it is placed before *Georges*. In standard French prosody, this final *e* would be voiced or pronounced only when it falls before a voiced consonant. Other syllabic elements analyzed here carry semantic value, as will be brought out later: *je* (I) and *or* (gold).—Trans.

11. I.e., "lui tiennent au corps." Another idiomatic expression is being detoured here: "tenir au coeur," to be held dear, close to someone's heart. The revision is motivated no doubt by the syllable *or* in "corps," body.—Trans.

12. Let it be said that Philippe's analysis occurred before Gilbert Bécaud's song "L'important, c'est la rose" had become popular.

13. "Gorge," which commonly means "throat," is also a classic euphemism for a woman's breasts.—Trans.

14. This name has also been transposed, according to the criteria already mentioned, so as to maintain both veiling and transgression.

15. This phrase includes an untranslatable pun: "qui ne trouve son re-

père que dans le nom." The term "repère," landmark, is here being recycled to indicate also a "re-father," a repeat father.—Trans.

Chapter 6

1. The study of logical articulations requires, in my opinion, that one take into consideration the nature of the articulations in play in the unconscious system, at least so as to specify the relation of exclusion that these latter articulations imply with regard to a subjective function.

2. Jean Laplanche writes: "This ballast that removes language from the exclusive reign of the primary processes . . . is precisely the existence of the unconscious chain" ("L'inconscient, une étude psychanalytique," in *L'inconscient*, p. 116).

3. See Victor Tausk, "On the Origin of the 'Influencing Machine' in Schizophrenia," in *The Psycho-Analytic Reader*, ed. Robert Fliess (New York: International Universities Press, 1967).

4. See Chapters 3 and 7.

5. See Chapter 3.

6. On this subject, see Jacques-Alain Miller, "La suture: Eléments de la logique du signifiant," in *Cahiers pour l'analyse* 1–2 (Jan. 1966): 46–49.

7. On this "eclipse of the subject," see, among other texts, Lacan, "Subversion of the Subject," pp. 314–15; on "vacillation," see as well Jean-Claude Milner, "Le Point du signifiant," in *Cahiers pour l'analyse* 3 (May 1966): 77.

8. "But we must insist that *jouissance* is forbidden to him who speaks as such, or else it can only be said between the lines," Lacan, "Subversion of the Subject," p. 319; translation modified.

9. On the psychoanalytic use of this French term, see Chapter 1, n. 22.—Trans.

10. See Lacan, "Subversion of the Subject": "The subjection of the subject to the signifier, which occurs in the circuit that goes from $s(O)$ to O and back from O to $s(O)$, is really a circle, inasmuch as the assertion that is established in it—for lack of being able to end on anything other than its own scansion . . . refers only to its own anticipation in the composition of the signifier, in itself insignificant" (p. 304, translation modified). On the "circular relation, or the reciprocal engendering of signifier-subject," see also Miller, "La suture," pp. 49–51.

11. On this subject, see the observation of Emmanuel, in X. Audouard, "Un Enfant exposé aux symboles," in *Recherches* (Sept. 1967): 147–71.

12. The term *thing* occurs to me here as regards the object. The possible relation between this use and the use Lacan makes of the term, beginning in "The Freudian Thing" (in *Ecrits: A Selection*) up to the evocation of the *agalma*, would have to be clarified.

13. See Chapter 3.

14. See Chapter 4.

15. "The Unconscious," *SE* 14: 186–87; *GW* 10: 285–86.

16. See M. Séchehaye, *La réalisation symbolique* (Bern: H. Hüber, 1947).

17. It would be more strictly correct to say *four* terms inasmuch as *one* letter implies at least *two*.

18. One will recognize in this question a personal approach to the Lacanian notion of the "great Other" or "O," in the sense that we retain only its definition, for example: "*O is the locus of the signifier's treasure*, which does not mean the code's treasure, for it is not that the univocal correspondence of a sign with something is preserved in it, but that the signifier is constituted only from a synchronic and enumerable collection of elements in which each is sustained only by the principle of its opposition to each of the others" (Lacan, "Subversion of the Subject," p. 304).

Chapter 7

1. Freud, "On the History of the Psycho-Analytic Movement," *SE* 14: 16; *GW* 10: 54.

2. See Chapter 3.

3. The expression "defile of the letter" echoes Lacan's use of the phrase "defile of the signifier" in several essays in the *Ecrits*. These texts make apparent that, for Lacan, the expression "defile of the signifier" characterizes in an imagistic way the formative effect of the prevalence of the signifying order. For example: "Man is, already before his birth and beyond his death, caught in the symbolic chain . . . in the play of the signifier" ("Situation de la psychanalyse en 1956," *Ecrits*, p. 468); "language and its structure exist prior to the moment at which each subject at a certain point in his mental development makes his entry into it" ("The Agency of the Letter in the Unconscious, or Reason Since Freud," in *Ecrits: A Selection*, p. 148); "the mother's omnipotence . . . not only suspends the satisfaction of needs from the signifying apparatus, but also . . . fragments them, filters them, models them upon the defiles of the structure of the signifier" ("The Direction of the Treatment and the Principles of Its Power," in *Ecrits: A Selection*, p. 255).

The use I am making here of the metaphor of the defile with regard to the thetic function differs perceptibly from the Lacanian use in that it accentuates the other extreme of the defile: that point at which the trait regulates the flow of *jouissance*, or even dams it up.

4. The notion of an absent or weak conscious organization should not be assimilated too hastily to the classic notions in psychoanalysis of "strong ego" and "weak ego."

5. "We have reason to assume that there is a *primal repression*, a first phase of repression, which consists in the psychical (ideational) representative [*Vorstellungs-Repräsentanz*] of the instinct being denied entrance into the conscious. With this a *fixation* is established; the representative in question persists unaltered from then onwards and the instinct remains attached to it," *SE* 14: 148; *GW* 10: 250.

6. See Chapter 6.

7. This formula is given in the original as $F_u - F_a$, which would indicate "fossette de l'un et fossette de l'autre," that is, "dimple of the one and dimple of the other," which seems incorrect here.—Trans.

8. The original reads, once again: $F_u - F_a$ (see preceding note).—Trans.

9. *Infans* should be understood literally as "the one who does not speak."

10. See Chapter 3.

11. Pierre Grimal, *The Dictionary of Classical Mythology*, trans. A. R. Maxwell-Hyslop (New York: Basil Blackwell, 1986), p. 456.

Chapter 8

1. Raymond Queneau, *Courir les rues* (Paris: Gallimard, 1967), p. 48. [The Cherche-Midi was an infamous prison in Paris. Its name means literally "look-for-noon." These lines play on a common French saying: "to look for noon at four o'clock," that is, to complicate things, to look for complications.—Trans.]

2. "The subject is only a subject by being the synchronic subjection in the field of the Other" (Lacan, unpublished seminar, May 20, 1964); "The traumatic, irreducible signifier, to which the subject is subjected" (ibid., June 17, 1964).

3. We should note that Lacan has on occasion characterized the analyst's desire as the desire to obtain absolute difference (unpublished seminar, June 24, 1964).

4. In the French, the "secondary letter" or "cipher" is coded as "G.L.B.," which stands for "guetter le gibier." This letter combination is

phonetically closer to the primary formula P.J.L. than are the initials of the translation, L.F.G.—Trans.

5. We cannot fail to underscore in passing, as we neglected to do in the analysis of the dream, the figuration-reproduction of my name in the theme of the "clearing [*clairière*]."

6. See Chapter 7.

7. We intersect in this manner with Lacan's formula, which characterizes the phallus as "signifier of the lack of the signifier" (unpublished seminar, Apr. 12, 1961). On this subject, see Lacan, "The Signification of the Phallus," in *Ecrits: A Selection*, p. 288, and "Subversion of the Subject," ibid., p. 319.

8. Freud, "On the Sexual Theories of Children," *SE* 9, 215; *GW* 7: 178.

9. Freud, "Analysis Terminable and Interminable," *SE* 23: 250–53; *GW* 16: 97–98.

10. Freud, "Analysis of a Phobia in a Five-Year-Old Boy," *SE* 10: 8, n. 2; *GW*, 7: 246, n. 1.

11. Alone inasmuch as the breast, which could also take the place of differential term, cannot be considered "lacking" in the man in the same way as the penis in the woman.

M E R I D I A N

Crossing Aesthetics

Library of Congress Cataloging-in-Publication Data

Leclaire, Serge.
    [Psychoanalyser.   English]
    Psychoanalyzing : on the order of the unconscious and the
practice of the letter / Serge Leclaire ; translated by Peggy Kamuf.
        p.   cm. — (Meridian: crossing aesthetics)
    Includes bibliographical references.
    ISBN 0-8047-2910-7 (alk. paper). — ISBN 0-8047-2911-5
(pbk. : alk. paper)
    1. Psychoanalysis.   2. Lacan, Jacques, 1901– .
I. Title.   II. Series: Meridian (Stanford, Calif.)
BF175.L413   1998
150.19'5—dc21   97-21856
                                                            CIP

⊗ This book is printed on acid-free, recycled paper.

Original printing 1998
Last figure below indicates year of this printing:
07   06   05   04   03   02   01   00   99   98